The New York Times

TAKE IT EASY CROSSWORD PUZZLES

The New York Times

TAKE IT EASY CROSSWORD PUZZLES
75 Easy Puzzles

Edited by Will Shortz

ST. MARTIN'S GRIFFIN ❧ NEW YORK

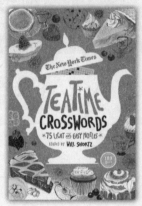

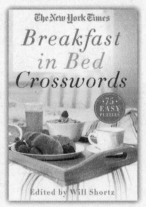

ACROSS

1 Name of five Norwegian kings
5 Words after work or museum
10 Former Iranian leader
14 How Charles Lindbergh flew across the Atlantic
15 French department capital known in Roman times as Nemausus
16 ___ Nostra (crime group)
17 Rock and roll has one in Cleveland
19 Pro's opposite
20 Org. that monitors gun sales
21 Reached
22 Shop employee
23 Words of greeting
26 Chandon's partner in Champagne
27 Blossom-to-be
28 October birthstone
30 Play, as a guitar
33 Dem.'s counterpart
36 1980s cop show that TV Guide once ranked as the greatest TV drama of all time
40 Dollar bill
41 Robber
42 Singer Fitzgerald
43 Battery for a TV remote
44 Window unit
46 James Earl Jones or Tommy Lee Jones
53 Zones
54 String quartet instrument
55 An evergreen
57 Gentlemen
58 Ruckus
60 Made off with
61 Freezing rain
62 Mexico's ___ California

63 One-named New Age singer
64 Succinctly put
65 What the Ugly Duckling became

DOWN

1 Worker protection org.
2 Reluctant (to)
3 Like the band Josie and the Pussycats
4 Stereo control: Abbr.
5 Walking
6 Saks ___ Avenue
7 Former Italian P.M. whose name means "beloved"
8 Cut again, as grass
9 China's Mao ___-tung
10 Reduced, with "back"
11 Beehive product
12 Houston player
13 Poem like "The swallow flies up / Into a blue evening sky, / Summer's small herald"
18 Devour with the eyes
22 Cookie morsel
24 Laze
25 Share a border with
28 "Well, what have we here!"
29 Brooch
30 ___ Lanka
31 Item in a golfer's pocket
32 B-ball official
33 Alternative to arbitrary governance
34 Wriggly fish
35 Smokey Bear ad, e.g., for short
37 Doesn't leave
38 Deice

39 Gave for a while
43 State that the Arctic Circle passes through
44 Aesthetic taste
45 "Call me ___!" "O.K., you're . . . !"
46 Proverbial waste maker
47 Heavenly hunter
48 "Bad, bad" Brown of song
49 Small egg
50 Houston player, once
51 Metes (out)
52 Spanish wine region, with "La"
56 Horse whose coat is sprinkled with white hairs
58 F.D.R.'s successor
59 "Six-pack" muscles

by Brent Sverdloff and Michael Blake

2

ACROSS

1 Helps
5 __-size model
9 Things
14 Licentious man
15 Paying close attention
16 __ congestion (cold symptom)
17 Small, cute residence?
19 Bygone Toyota sports car
20 Music with conga drums
21 500 sheets of paper
23 Moral toughness
24 Device for killing mosquitoes?
27 Annie who was nicknamed "Little Sure Shot"
31 Like a well-worn dirt road
32 Pouring into a shot glass, e.g.?
36 Come to earth
37 Fair-hiring inits.
38 Stars and __ (Confederate flag)
42 Relatives of slack jaws?
46 Delilah was his undoing
50 "Stop joshin' me!"
51 What wakes everyone up in the morning at the duck pond?
55 Sch. for future admirals
56 Like books and tea leaves
57 Host at a roast
62 "Ad __ per aspera" (Kansas' motto)
64 Archenemy of Bugs Bunny . . . who might say things like 17-, 24-, 32-, 42- and 51-Across
66 Wail of an ambulance
67 Den
68 Not __ deal

69 Having an exhilarating effect
70 Trig function
71 Leave completely filled

DOWN

1 Counterpart of sciences
2 Des Moines's home
3 Fight at 20 paces, say
4 Lays eyes on
5 Expert
6 Advice-giving "Dr." of radio
7 Surprise victory
8 Sauna feature
9 Shoo-__ (overwhelming favorites)
10 Instructed
11 __ de corps
12 Jarhead
13 On the schedule
18 Goalie Dominik with 16 seasons in the N.H.L.
22 Man's nickname that's just wonderful?
25 Letter before zee
26 Signal from offstage
27 __ exams (tests at the end of a student's fifth year at Hogwarts)
28 "Eureka!"
29 Family relations
30 "Acid"
33 Wood for archery bows
34 One of the Stooges
35 U.K. lexicon
38 Software problem
39 From __ Z
40 Letter before sigma
41 Fig. on an application
42 Stir-fry vessel

43 __ about (approximately)
44 Gaping opening
45 Proprietor
46 Racket sport
47 Sydneysider, for one
48 Words said over and over
49 Chicken
52 Believes
53 __ Lama
54 PC network overseer
58 Degs. for creative types
59 Country with which the U.S. re-established diplomatic relations in 2015
60 Toolbar heading
61 Narrow advantage
63 "__ last words?"
65 Before, to poets

by Daniel Larsen

ACROSS

1 Sunrise
5 Musial in the Baseball Hall of Fame
9 High in the air
14 Soil-related prefix
15 Diva's solo
16 Stubble remover
17 Only president to scale the Matterhorn
19 Love, to Lorenzo
20 Temporary
21 Fine, thin cotton fabric
23 Bill ___, the Science Guy
24 Cheer (for)
26 Women's stockings
27 Only president whose grandfather was also president
29 Move like a bunny
32 Space streakers
35 Moms
36 Had on
37 Only president born outside the continental United States
38 Bo or Checkers
39 Only president to have 15 children
40 Photos, informally
41 Make a quick note of, with "down"
42 Writer Hemingway
43 Airport pickup driver's info
44 Only president to be a lifelong bachelor
46 Mend, as socks
48 Cheerleader's cheer
49 Lead-in to historic
52 Washington's Union ___
55 TV ratings name
57 Former Afghan leader Karzai
58 Only president to be married in the White House
60 Submit a tax return online
61 End in ___ (require overtime)
62 Marc Antony's lover, informally
63 Sports figures?
64 Building annex: Abbr.
65 Eurasian duck

DOWN

1 "Mack the Knife" singer Bobby
2 Excruciating pain
3 Worked on an essay or novel
4 Scent picker-upper
5 Redeemers
6 Sign of an earthquake
7 Be sick
8 Defense alliance since 1949, for short
9 Catherine of ___
10 Tibetan priests
11 Seasonal thinning in the atmosphere over Antarctica
12 Only president to serve as both vice president and president without being elected to either office
13 Card that just beats a deuce
18 Printing mistakes
22 Greek P's
25 Dalton who played 007
27 ___ and haws
28 Give in to gravity
30 Iron and tin sources
31 Saucy
32 Deal (with)
33 Last words?
34 Nut from Hawaii
36 Vegas casino developer Steve
38 Bespectacled Disney dwarf
39 Tourist destination in County Kerry, Ireland
41 Roman goddess, protector of women and marriage
42 Jazz up
44 Wedding figures
45 Epic poem starting with the flight from Troy
47 Slanted
49 Sacred song
50 Soprano Fleming
51 Fund, as a university chair
52 Tom Jones's "___ a Lady"
53 Only president to administer the oath of office to two other presidents
54 March Madness org.
56 Legal entities for partnerships: Abbr.
59 Inc., overseas

by Ed Stein and Paula Gamache

4

ACROSS

1 Plants used to make tequila
7 Health resort amenity
10 Penne ___ vodka
14 Flying insect with prominent eyespots
15 University address ender
16 Painful muscle injury
17 Frozen CO_2, familiarly
18 Grooming accessory that may be stuck in the hair
20 Classic American dessert
22 Lays out neatly
23 Granola morsel
24 Tenant
26 "___ already said too much"
28 Smaller cousin of the double bass
30 Would-be attorneys' hurdles, briefly
34 Qatari capital
36 Like some profs.
37 Frame job
38 Cass of the Mamas & the Papas
40 Obi-Wan ___ (Jedi knight)
41 Taking no guff
42 Spitting sound
45 Federal tax agts.
46 Rain delay covers
47 Undergoes oxidation
49 Driver's licenses and such, for short
50 BlackBerry alternative
52 Sans prescription, in brief
54 Washington and environs, informally
57 Material to sketch on
61 Michael Corleone player in "The Godfather"
63 Relating to songbirds
64 Take care of, as the bill
65 Ornamental pond fish
66 Trade associations
67 Genre
68 "www" address
69 Exam for an ambitious H.S. student . . . or what this puzzle has been?

DOWN

1 Opera set in Egypt
2 Trail mix
3 "Parks and Recreation" star
4 "And there it is!"
5 "And so on and so forth"
6 Generic name for a herding dog
7 Congers, e.g.
8 Sharable PC file
9 Invisible emanations
10 Currently
11 ___ Organa ("Star Wars" princess)
12 Having an open, delicate pattern
13 Chests in synagogues
19 Ultimatum's end
21 Societal troubles
25 Barfly
26 Explanatory Latin phrase
27 Physicist Alessandro, inventor of the electric battery
29 Grab a bite
31 Nuclear reactor
32 Went leisurely downriver, perhaps
33 Recasts damaging information in a favorable light, say
35 Plane hijacker
39 How freelance work is typically done
40 Pup : wolf :: ___ : fox
42 Expert
43 Source of healthful fatty acids in a StarKist can
44 Exploiter
48 Absorbs, as gravy
51 5-7-5 verse
53 Wordlessly implied
54 Batty
55 Sicken with sentiment
56 Per person
58 Garment draped over the shoulders
59 Draws to a close
60 Be at leisure
62 Neither here ___ there

by Timothy Polin

ACROSS

1. "No problem for me!"
6. Peru's capital
10. Omar of Fox's "House"
14. Dickens's "___ House"
15. Per item
16. Hand lotion ingredient
17. Intimidates, in a way
19. Crime scene barrier
20. Goes to, as a meeting
21. Not as hard
23. Airport up the coast from LAX
24. Flash mobs, once
25. "Science Guy" Bill
26. Jean ___, father of Dadaism
29. "Oh, darn!"
32. Fired (up)
34. Period between wars
36. Goat's cry
37. World's fair, for short
38. Circus animals that balance beach balls on their noses
40. "When You Wish ___ a Star"
43. Manning who was twice Super Bowl M.V.P.
45. Watch or clock
47. Showed in syndication, say
49. Justice Kagan
50. Numbered hwy.
51. Abbr. before a credit card date
52. Feeling blue
54. ___ card (cellphone chip)
56. Exercise in a pool
58. Cross-reference for further information
62. Male deer
63. On a lower floor
66. "___ kleine Nachtmusik"
67. "Ars Amatoria" poet
68. Foe
69. Ones in suits?
70. Big name in pet food
71. Aid in storm-tracking

DOWN

1. "2 Broke Girls" airer
2. Ski area near Salt Lake City
3. "Cool!"
4. Pub game
5. Artist Georgia who is known for her flower canvases
6. Cheryl of "Charlie's Angels"
7. Wall St. debuts
8. Trim the lawn
9. Sleeper's problem
10. Has supper
11. Unlined sheets without any writing
12. Sailor who's smitten by Olive Oyl
13. Get angry
18. Pig noses
22. Name first encountered in Genesis 2
24. "Understand?," slangily
26. Big galoot
27. Tyrannosaurus ___
28. Classroom missile
30. Followed a weight-loss plan
31. Alternative to AOL or Yahoo
33. Island ESE of Oahu
35. Pepsi, for one
39. Just knows
41. Month before Nov.
42. Born: Fr.
44. Police dept. figure
46. Van Gogh or Van Dyck
47. Moses parted it
48. Beautifully strange
53. "Me, too"
55. 2016 Disney film set in Polynesia
57. 10 and 8 for Bart and Lisa Simpson, respectively
58. Do the breaststroke, e.g.
59. Terminals
60. Like the score 7-7
61. Humorous Bombeck
64. Lab eggs
65. Damascus's land: Abbr.

by Zhouqin Burnikel

6

ACROSS

1 ___ jacket (bit of casualwear)
5 Dish that's sometimes rated in "alarms"
10 Curds and ___
14 Wagon part
15 Like much music
16 In fine fettle
17 Widespread
18 1960s activist Hoffman
19 Has
20 ___ friends (not having to be on one's guard)
22 Quaint inn, informally
24 Cry after "Ready!"
25 Muffed one
27 Bearlike
29 Powerful Renaissance family
32 A book collector might seek a first one
33 Available
34 Spanish girlfriend
35 Italy's shape
36 Setting for much of the movie "Lion"
38 Zippo
42 People encountered by Pizarro
44 Things ghosts lack
46 Riga native
49 Charms
50 In addition
51 What tryptophan is said to induce
52 Place to go for a "me day"
53 Munchkins
55 Nash who wrote "Parsley / Is gharsley"
59 Turner or Fey
61 Bother greatly
63 Tell to "Do it!"
64 Lead-in to a conclusion
65 Movie, informally
66 Class with mats
67 Feature of a late-night show set
68 Words to live by
69 Catch sight of

DOWN

1 Morning joe
2 Start of many a doctor's visit
3 In addition
4 Outcome that's overall unfavorable
5 Windy City 'L' overseer
6 Imaginary tiger friend in the comics
7 Not on good terms (with)
8 Done nothing
9 Infamous prison featured in the 1969 best seller "Papillon"
10 "___ knew?"
11 Southernmost U.S. state
12 Weather concern in 11-Down
13 Lackeys
21 Sheepish look
23 Two-masted vessel
26 Socialist Workers Party's ideology
28 Honest sorts . . . or what the circled squares contain?
29 Palindromic boy's name
30 "Be My Yoko ___" (first single by Barenaked Ladies)
31 Pi's follower
32 Former Big Four record co.
34 They're taken out in newspapers
37 Palindromic girl's name
39 Lungful
40 Hollywood ending?
41 Nincompoop
43 River that feeds Lake Nasser
45 Topping in kosher restaurants
46 Didn't run out
47 Have dreams
48 Features of some country singers
49 Region on the Rhine
51 Took effect
54 Area between mountains
56 Plunge
57 Breakfast food with a rhyming slogan
58 In order
60 Totally fine
62 Box office purchase: Abbr.

by Jacob Stulberg

ACROSS

1 Medicine-approving org.
4 Wine barrel
8 Awards in the ad biz
13 Rainbow shape
14 Opera melody
15 Quick look
16 Paving goo
17 Article of outerwear for an urbanite?
19 Too many of them "spoil the broth"
21 Bunny's movement
22 Component of a science course
23 Article of outerwear for a champagne drinker?
26 Done: Fr.
27 Having a ho-hum attitude
28 Warm greeting
29 Justice Sotomayor
30 Leave full
31 Common weather phenomenon in San Francisco
32 Ankle-high work shoe
33 Article of outerwear for a candy lover?
36 Potato chips, to Brits
39 ___-rock (music genre)
40 Entree that may be slathered in barbecue sauce
44 "Grand" women
45 Classic muscle car
46 Removes the rind from
47 Inlets
48 Article of outerwear for a housekeeper?
50 Lee who directed "Life of Pi"
51 ___ Harbour, Fla.
52 Newspapers, collectively
53 Article of outerwear for a General Motors employee?

57 Bird that gives a hoot
59 Gold standards
60 ___ lily
61 Chinese leader with a Little Red Book
62 Panache
63 Rat or roach
64 No. after a main telephone no.

DOWN

1 What the "Gras" of Mardi Gras means
2 Count with fangs
3 Circus tumbler
4 Witch's laugh
5 Crop up
6 Command to a dog
7 Mary ___ cosmetics
8 Bit from a movie
9 Fond du ___, Wis.
10 Faintest idea
11 Easter Island locale
12 Belgrade native
15 Unappetizing food that might be served with a ladle
18 Carpet variety
20 Thinks, thinks, thinks (about)
23 Small ammo
24 Command spoken while pulling the reins
25 Rambunctious little kids
26 200- or 400-meter run, e.g.
29 Madrid Mrs.
31 N.F.L. three-pointers: Abbr.
32 Droid
34 Alternative to FedEx
35 Thicken, as blood
36 Holders of some music collections

37 Headgear for a drizzly day
38 Descriptive language
41 Annoying
42 Honeycomb product
43 Retired jet, for short
45 Shorebird with a distinctive shriek
46 Caged talker
48 Painters' touches
49 Some computer picture files
51 Memory unit
54 Kilmer of "Top Gun"
55 Nile viper
56 Middle of Arizona?
58 Auction grouping

by Susan Gelfand

8

ACROSS

1 Things that may be displayed on a general's chest
7 "Oh no!," in comics
10 Old Testament prophet
14 "Leave this to me!"
15 West who said "It's better to be looked over than overlooked"
16 Foreign Legion hat
17 Famously unfinished 14th-century literary work, with "The"
20 Hotel name synonymous with poshness
21 Org. whose motto is "We are their voice"
22 Historical period
23 "Happy Days" diner
24 "How cheap!"
27 Exam for the college-bound, for short
29 Reggae relative
30 What one might start over with
35 Arthur Ashe Stadium org.
39 Prevents litter?
40 Beverage that may be 41-Across
41 Alternative to "bottled"
42 "Shame on you!" sounds
43 Losing crunchiness, as chips
45 Ukr., e.g., once
47 Org.'s cousin
48 Historical figure played by David Bowie in "The Prestige"
54 Narcotics-fighting grp.
57 Rapid-fire gun
58 Embellish
59 Uphill aid for skiers
60 "Finally . . ."
64 Cut with a beam
65 Sighs of relief
66 Some family reunion attendees
67 ___ terrier
68 Tennis do-over
69 Like wind chimes

DOWN

1 Millionths of a meter
2 Spam medium
3 "Shhh!"
4 Movie that came out about the same time as "A Bug's Life"
5 Emulate Pinocchio
6 Orch. section
7 Something necessary
8 Gripes
9 It's just for openers
10 Letters on a "Wanted" poster
11 Major scuffle
12 Sydney ___ House
13 Agave fiber used in rugs
18 Sheep sound
19 Job to do
24 Catches some rays
25 Altitudes: Abbr.
26 Gibes
28 States positively
30 Winter hrs. in Texas
31 The Stones' "12 × 5" and "Flowers"
32 Chinese philosopher ___-tzu
33 "___ Baba and the Forty Thieves"
34 Full complement of bowling pins
36 "Give him some space!"
37 Chess champ Mikhail
38 Copy
41 Bones, anatomically
43 Done bit by bit
44 Half of a square dance duo
46 Chunk of concrete
48 Makes void
49 ___ Walton League (conservation group)
50 Given to smooching
51 ___ nth degree
52 Dadaist Max
53 Lead-in to Cat or cone
55 Prop found near a palette
56 ___-craftsy
59 27-Across taker, typically
61 Shape of a three-way intersection
62 Channel with explosive content?
63 52, in old Rome

by Freddie Cheng

ACROSS

1 Lawyer: Abbr.
5 British sports car, briefly
8 What ignorance is, they say
13 One might end "Q.E.D."
15 A pitcher wants a low one, for short
16 "___ One: A Star Wars Story"
17 Atlantic site of strange disappearances
20 Michael who played both Batman and Birdman
21 Aid for a lost driver, for short
22 Big laugh
23 Russian jet
24 Former British P.M. Tony
26 "As is" transaction
30 Frank of the Mothers of Invention
34 WSW's opposite
35 Jazzy Fitzgerald
36 Colorful aquarium swimmers
37 "___ my words"
39 You are here
41 Didn't float
42 Like zombies
44 Cause for being refused a drink at a bar
46 Opposite of bright
47 Four-time M.L.B. All-Star José
48 Excellent service
50 Terse
52 "That feels so-o-o-o nice!"
53 Halloween's mo.
56 Amazement
57 Water down
60 Punny description for 17-, 26- or 48-Across
64 Boredom
65 Sup
66 Florida senator Marco
67 Band with the 2000 hit "Bye Bye Bye"
68 Just for Men offering
69 Treaty

DOWN

1 Alert to squad cars, for short
2 Arduous walk
3 Ripped
4 Start of a playground joke
5 Denim fabric
6 Trump's "The ___ of the Deal"
7 Use Listerine, say
8 Victoria's Secret measurement
9 Chaney of horror
10 Azalea of rap
11 Lieutenant on the original U.S.S. Enterprise
12 "___ and ye shall find"
14 Hopeless
18 Iditarod vehicle
19 Hoppy brew, for short
24 Nonsense, as the Irish might say
25 "Darn!"
26 Leg bone connected to the knee bone
27 Stupid
28 Passionately brainy, say
29 Chicken ___ king
31 Fashion house founded in Milan
32 Emotion causing hyperventilation
33 "___ Another" (NPR game show)
36 It's in the stratosphere
38 Hold on to
40 Weight unit on a bridge sign
43 From east of the Urals
45 One placing a telephone call
48 Organization for Janet Yellen, informally
49 "Button your lip!"
51 Tango requirement
53 Store sign that might be flipped at 9 a.m.
54 Inmates
55 Wee
57 Lavish care (on)
58 Instrument that makes the cheeks puff out
59 Clapton who sang "Layla"
61 Habit wearer
62 "No" vote
63 "Just kidding!"

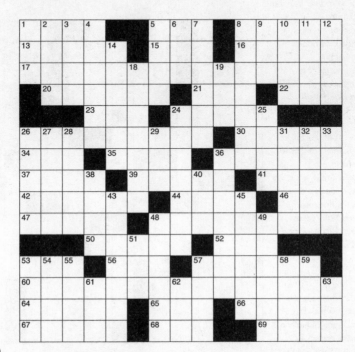

by Alan DeLoriea

ACROSS

1 Pop fan?
4 Numbers to crunch
8 Asian gambling mecca
13 Singer DiFranco
14 Water pitchers
16 Slender woodwinds
17 Asian electronics giant
18 Mystery writer Marsh
19 Sporty car in a Beach Boys song
20 *"It's a Mad, Mad, Mad, Mad World" actor, 1963
22 Year, south of the border
23 A pep talk might boost it
24 *"12 Angry Men" actor, 1957
28 Reduce to particles
30 Online money transfer facilitator
31 Scruff of the neck
32 Made bird noises
35 Pig's digs
36 *"Anatomy of a Murder" actor, 1959
40 "Breaking Bad" network
43 It's a size larger than grande at Starbucks
44 Sounds of satisfaction
48 Like a toasted marshmallow vis-à-vis a non-toasted one
50 Shirt with straps instead of sleeves
53 *"Road Trip" actor, 2000
56 Rice-based Spanish dish
57 PC "brain"
58 Youthful time in one's life . . . which this puzzle might harken solvers back to?
60 Did a smith's job on
62 Prized violin
63 D.C. ballplayer
64 In and of itself
65 Mister, south of the border
66 Prefix with borough
67 Bohemian
68 Puts in stitches
69 Dog breeder's org.

DOWN

1 One admired for his masculinity
2 The tiniest bit
3 Gesture to punctuate a great performance
4 Highest mountain in North America
5 "What a bummer!"
6 Oolong and Earl Grey
7 Popular typeface
8 Bon ___ (witticism)
9 Monastic realm
10 Many washers and dryers in apartment buildings
11 Stunt pilot
12 Amer. money
15 Peeved
21 Hitchcock role in almost every Hitchcock film
25 Sporting sword
26 Actress ___ Pinkett Smith
27 Journalist Nellie
29 "Micro" and "macro" subject, for short
33 Province west of Que.
34 Passing mention?
37 Winnebago owner, briefly
38 Bone-dry
39 In the buff
40 F.B.I. employee: Abbr.
41 Sponge
42 Behave
45 1996 Olympics site
46 It stores a synagogue's Torah scrolls
47 Moving jerkily
49 "Um . . . O.K."
51 "Superbad" producer Judd
52 Low points
54 Those, to José
55 April, May and June, for example
59 Swimmer's assignment
60 Where you might hear 44-Across
61 Susan of "L.A. Law"

by Damon J. Gulczynski

Note: This collaboration is by the astrophysicist Neil deGrasse Tyson and his Harvard classmate Andrea Carla Michaels (with her 56th puzzle for The Times).

ACROSS

1 Fix, as a cat
5 "Get cracking!"
9 "Jurassic Park" insect casing
14 Pack animal
15 "___ girl!"
16 First lady after Hillary
17 "That's my cue!"
18 Like Dorothy's slippers
19 Boston airport
20 Toe testing the waters?
23 Potentially dangerous bacterium
24 ExxonMobil?
28 "___ Comedy Jam"
29 Command to Rover
32 "Bald-faced" thing
33 "Who goes there, friend or ___?"
34 Bowling scoresheet unit
36 Square dance site
37 Oscar nominees' gathering?
41 Vittles
43 Manipulate, as bread dough
44 Bird that hoots
45 Mai ___ (cocktail)
48 Admit, with "up to"
49 '50s high school dance
52 Bashful?
55 Inventory items
57 Total hottie?
60 Simple pond life
63 "Me as well"
64 "Voulez-vous coucher ___ moi ce soir?"
65 It may be reasonable to a jury
66 Catches forty winks
67 Intertwine
68 New Mexican pueblo builders
69 Exuberance
70 Regarding, in a memo

DOWN

1 Wore an upside-down frown
2 Volcanic rock
3 Many, many
4 1983 film in which Barbra Streisand dresses as a man
5 Suffix with million
6 ___ poker
7 Equally large
8 E-commerce site formerly owned by eBay
9 Declare to be true
10 Native New Zealanders
11 Computer program glitch
12 Paleozoic or Mesozoic
13 Sought political office
21 "The Scales" constellation
22 Greek letter before omega
25 Quite a distance off
26 Neither's partner
27 Hamilton's bill
30 Body part to lend or bend
31 Big inits. in trucks
34 1-800-FLOWERS alternative
35 Certain fraternal order member
36 Place to dream
37 Successful auctioneer's last word
38 Commercial game with wild cards
39 Put in stitches
40 Having an aftertaste, as some barbecue sauce
41 Debate position against "against"
42 Have debts
45 140-character messages
46 Drivers' org.
47 John who wrote "The World According to Garp"
49 Reindeer feet
50 Most bizarre
51 1960 Alfred Hitchcock thriller
53 Abu ___ (Mideast land)
54 Prebirth
56 President who won the 2009 Nobel Peace Prize
58 "Ain't happening"
59 Finish second
60 Woodworking tool
61 Baseballer Gehrig
62 Rifle or revolver

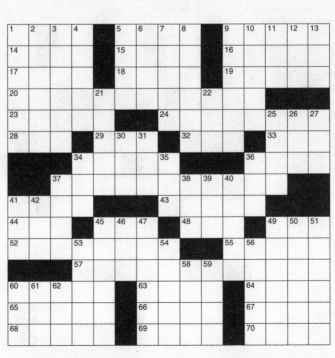

by Neil deGrasse Tyson and Andrea Carla Michaels

ACROSS

1 Work like Dürer
5 Peter or Paul, but not Mary
9 Bath fixture
14 Lilting melodies
15 Concerning, to a lawyer
16 Musical with the song "Don't Cry for Me Argentina"
17 Trick football play
20 ___ bark beetle
21 One side of a debate
22 Dude, Jamaica-style
23 Office staple since the 1980s
30 Birth control method, for short
31 Peach or plum
32 Descartes's "therefore"
33 Super Bowl-winning QB Bart
36 Bollywood soundtrack instrument
38 ". . . man ___ mouse?"
39 High-ranking British Parliament member
42 Doctors' org.
43 Something one shouldn't make in public
44 Lifesavers for cops and sailors
45 Disposable lighters and pens
47 The mark of Zorro
48 You, abroad
49 Floor warning
55 Good noise from an engine
56 Sarcastic laugh sound
57 Green govt. group
58 Study at a college that doesn't have applications?
64 Seize without legal authority
65 Listening device
66 Ink stain
67 Pool contents?
68 Newspaper essay
69 Old one, in Oldenburg

DOWN

1 Alleviated
2 Duke or dame
3 Pulls an all-nighter, say
4 "The buck stops here" prez
5 Bar on a car
6 Be a busybody
7 Pound sound
8 Family member: Abbr.
9 Genre for Dizzy Gillespie and Charlie Parker
10 Way or means
11 Paul McCartney, for one
12 Onetime telecommunications conglomerate, for short
13 Opposing vote
18 Bullish trends
19 Bully's boast
24 Dame ___ Te Kanawa
25 Entrance for Santa
26 Navel formation?
27 Moves briskly
28 White heron
29 Surf sounds
33 Signs of healing
34 Native of southern India or northern Sri Lanka
35 You can count on them
36 It's no bull
37 Nice location
40 Itchy condition
41 Out in public
46 Baseball or basketball
48 Humiliated
50 Basketball inflaters
51 Invitation heading
52 "Mack the Knife" composer
53 Disney World theme park
54 It's often unaccounted for . . . or a hint to this puzzle's circled letters
58 Short-haired dog
59 Play for a patsy
60 7,485 performances, for Broadway's original "Cats"
61 Noah count?
62 With it
63 [No info yet]

by George Barany and John D. Child

ACROSS

1 Set of pictures at a dentist's
6 Crow's sound
9 Reprieves
15 Event for meeting new people
16 "I love," to Cato
17 Perfect world
18 "The one thing that's clear to me . . ."
20 Picked
21 Appear
22 "Smoking or ___?"
23 Boxing achievements, in brief
24 Distant
29 Narrow water passage
32 "___ day now . . ."
33 Villainous count in the Lemony Snicket books
35 Obama's successor
36 Jason's ship
37 Pull off perfectly
38 Many millennia
39 Police operation . . . or, when read another way, what a grammarian would like to do to 18-, 24-, 52- and 65-Across?
43 Day-___ paint
44 Japanese soup
46 Boaters' implements
47 Some woodwinds
49 Lose traction on the road
50 Vietnamese soup
51 What Google's Ngram program tracks, for word usage
52 Narrative connector
56 Peach pit or walnut
57 Greedy one
58 Peach or walnut
62 Cuba's capital
65 "What do you think of . . . ?"
67 Unscripted comedy, informally
68 Mimic
69 Watch over
70 Blue state?
71 Fluorescent bulb alternative, for short
72 Novices

DOWN

1 Dec. celebration
2 Tick off
3 What car wheels turn on
4 Polite affirmative
5 ___ Lanka
6 Group of books that an educated person is supposed to be familiar with
7 In the company of
8 Blow away
9 Jealous words of congratulations
10 Cultural spirit
11 "You can't joke about that yet"
12 FedEx rival
13 Thanksgiving dessert
14 ___ Juan, Puerto Rico
19 Problem with a shoelace
23 Dance in which one partner might hold a rose between his teeth
25 One might apply gloss to them
26 Things for sale
27 Old-fashioned wine holder
28 Unsuccessful
29 Thorny parts of roses
30 Group of three
31 Enters hurriedly
34 Often-unheeded advice from dentists
36 Ohio city that was once the Rubber Capital of the World
40 Liable to tip over, maybe
41 Expressed amazement
42 Labourite's opponent, in British politics
45 "Most likely . . ."
48 Big electronics chain
51 License plates
53 Choir member
54 "Fingers crossed!"
55 Planted, as discord
59 Sound to fear in the savanna
60 Currency of France or Italy
61 When planes are due to take off, for short
62 That guy
63 "What ___, chopped liver?"
64 Biden and Pence, in brief
65 Actor Holbrook
66 10%-er: Abbr.

by Tom McCoy

14

ACROSS

1 Even trade
5 Nile predator, briefly
9 Class with masks?
14 Next in line
15 Promise
16 18th-century mathematician who introduced the function
17 Designer Gucci
18 Nick at ___
19 One-named singer who won the 2016 Album of the Year
20 "Sorry I'm in your space, it's an actress thing," said ___
23 Shirt that might have a crew neck, informally
24 Scottish cap
25 "The Raven" writer's monogram
28 "Don't interrupt me on my radio show," said ___
32 "It gets better" spot, e.g., in brief
34 DiCaprio, to fans
35 Prefix with galactic and spatial
36 Works to get
39 Lion's prey
41 Easily fooled
42 Unit of bacon
43 Lennon's widow
45 ___-Mex
46 "Gotta run, pop concert calls," said ___
51 Turn-___
52 Gravestone letters
53 Govt. org. with a drone registry program
54 "Right to the point: You're beautiful, it's true," said ___
60 Advocated
63 Tea type
64 Three, in Berlin
65 Mecca resident
66 Drying oven
67 Harvest, as crops
68 "A man who, when he smells flowers, looks around for a coffin," per H. L. Mencken
69 Rice wine
70 Longings

DOWN

1 Carpet style
2 Word said three times before "What have we here?!"
3 Assistant
4 On the double
5 Hide
6 Inner part of a racetrack
7 Palindromic boy's name
8 Treasure holders
9 Request for a hand
10 Inspiring 1993 movie about a Notre Dame football team walk-on
11 Lager relative
12 Comical Brooks
13 "All we ___ saying is give peace a chance"
21 Just-made
22 Munch on
25 Thing that exists
26 Drug whose generic name is naproxen
27 Measuring cup material
28 Truman and others
29 Rule laid down by a commission: Abbr.
30 "What should I ___?"
31 Material in strands
32 Sauce with pine nuts
33 The Great Tempter
37 Zero, in soccer
38 Occasional
40 Prefix with -versal
44 Not connected to a computer network
47 Pacific ___
48 What stars are in the night sky
49 Letter after sigma
50 Tom who coached the Dallas Cowboys for 29 years
54 Revered "Star Wars" figure
55 Actor LaBeouf
56 Illegal pitching motion
57 Logician's chart
58 Not stand completely straight
59 Nervousness that causes a golfer to miss an easy putt, with "the"
60 Golden State sch.
61 With 62-Down, sci-fi weapon
62 See 61-Down

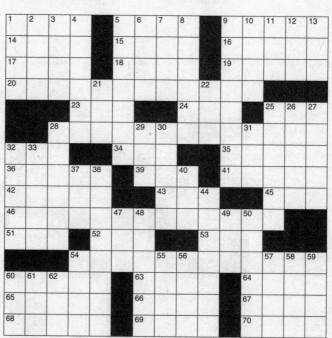

by Ryan Milligan

ACROSS

1 Inflated senses of self
5 Moisture in the air
10 Flower girl?
14 Muppet with a unibrow
15 Furious
16 The "N" of N.F.L.: Abbr.
17 Coating for fish that you might think would make you tipsy
19 Sound heard in a cave
20 "Cheers!," in Scandinavia
21 Historical periods
23 Derby or fedora
24 Cinderella's carriage
28 Hit the slopes
31 ___ v. Wade
32 Cousins of emus
33 Classical paintings
35 Org. that operates the Jupiter orbiter
38 ___-C.I.O.
39 Rough estimates . . . or what the ends of 17-, 24-, 52- and 65-Across are?
44 Slangy "sweetie"
45 Pepper's partner
46 California wine valley
47 Popular pain reliever
49 Have a part in a play
51 Talk, talk, talk
52 Waiter's refilling aid
57 Utmost
58 Sport for heavyweights
59 Curses (out)
63 Couple, in a gossip column
65 Overhead cooler
68 Ruler said to have fiddled while Rome burned
69 Superman's birth name
70 Song for a diva
71 Sprouted
72 Underhanded sort
73 Like marathons and maxiskirts

DOWN

1 Recedes, as the tide
2 Sheldon of "The Big Bang Theory," for one
3 Cookie that may be dipped in milk
4 Subway standee's support
5 By way of
6 Works at a museum
7 ___ Philippe (Swiss watchmaker)
8 Cheri formerly of "S.N.L"
9 Aired, as old TV shows
10 Suffix with serpent
11 Host of TV's "30 Minute Meals"
12 Cornell University's home
13 Tree huggers?
18 Fuzzy picture
22 One who's all skin and bones
25 Leonardo da Vinci's "___ Lisa"
26 Fruits that are a little grittier than apples
27 "That sounds good - NOT!"
28 Cry big tears
29 Maker of autodom's Optima
30 Words after "Reach Out" in a #1 Four Tops hit
34 Work like a dog
36 Cousin of calypso
37 Quacky insurance giant
40 House of Lords members
41 Scratch target
42 Pollution police, for short
43 Softhead
47 Store window shader
48 ___-day Saints (Mormons)
50 Fork-tailed bird
53 Hockey discs
54 "Wait, let me explain . . ."
55 French fabric
56 Majestic
60 Big, round head of hair
61 Street through the middle of town
62 Slight problem
64 Cut the lawn
66 Pasture
67 Kind

by Agnes Davidson and Zhouqin Burnikel

16

ACROSS

1 Defunct gridiron org.
4 Fireplace holder
9 Rather conservative
14 Chapter in history
15 Race with batons
16 Pink cocktail, informally
17 What zero bars on a cellphone indicates
19 Synthetic fabric
20 Old-fashioned theaters
21 "Memoirs of a Geisha" accessory
22 Bit of dinero
23 Viking tales, e.g.
28 "Shame on you!"
29 Ring decoration
30 Opposite of wane
31 Glowing coal
34 Like advice worth listening to
36 Leg-revealing item of apparel
37 Experts on the brain
40 "Shoot!"
41 Sour milk product
42 "Someone turn on a fan!"
43 Surgery locales, for short
44 Quick hit
45 Notch shape
46 Baseball, in America
53 Cross to bear
54 Puppy's plaint
55 Desktop image
56 Wisecracks
58 Disney character hinted at by the circled letters
60 Apply, as pressure
61 Opening remarks
62 Flood refuge
63 Refugee camp sights
64 Visibly stunned
65 ___ chi

DOWN

1 Fifth member in a noble line
2 Tolkien hero
3 Futuristic weapon
4 Canine warning
5 Uprising
6 "I was at the movies - nowhere near the crime," e.g.
7 Understood
8 Look over
9 1996 horror movie with three sequels
10 Done for
11 "Sure, go ahead"
12 Texter's qualifier
13 Mafia V.I.P.
18 Old airline with the slogan "We have to earn our wings every day"
22 Fuss over oneself
24 Modern prefix with skeptic
25 Urged (on)
26 Totaled, as a bill
27 Have life
31 Conclude with
32 Stiller's longtime wife and comedy partner
33 Explode
34 Recreational device that holds 35-Down
35 See 34-Down
36 Imitative
38 Reads carefully
39 Gets even with?
44 Renaissance Faire events
45 Steam and such
47 Sluggish
48 What causes the circled letters to grow?
49 Companion of the Niña and Santa Maria
50 Apple's former instant-messaging program
51 "On the Beach" heroine
52 Gourmet mushroom
56 Boeing product
57 Hacker, but not on a computer
58 ___ mater (brain cover)
59 Admit (to)

by Timothy Polin

ACROSS

1 Something to make before blowing out the birthday candles
5 Staple of Greek cuisine
9 All-knowing sort
14 ___ Morita, co-founder of Sony
15 ___ vera
16 Kind of bond in chemistry
17 What Thoreau lived in at Walden Pond
19 Romance or horror
20 Indian Ocean bloc?
22 Hibernation station
23 Measurements of 60-Acrosses
24 Central American bloc?
33 "I'm cool with that"
34 Brother in an order
35 Steel support for concrete
36 Letter insert: Abbr.
37 Non-Jew
39 Bill who popularizes science
40 Many, colloquially
42 Land of Donegal and Dingle Bay
43 Paula of "Paula's Home Cooking"
44 Western European bloc?
47 Multivolume ref.
48 Scottish cap
49 Organization founded in 1945 . . . or a literal description of 20-, 24- and 44-Across?
56 2008 movie with the line "I will find you, and I will kill you"
58 Softening-up words before a request
59 Prevent, as disaster
60 Alkali neutralizer
61 Mishmash
62 ___ profundo (lowest vocal range)

63 Motto for a modern risk-taker, for short
64 Email folder

DOWN

1 Insect with a hanging nest
2 Furnishings retailer with gigantic stores
3 "Awesome!"
4 Office-closing time
5 What phone books are alphabetized by
6 Inter ___
7 Apollo program destination
8 Mercedes-___
9 Words next to a dotted line
10 Cry of lament
11 Elsa's younger sister in "Frozen"
12 Russian space station
13 Diamonds, slangily
18 ___ interface
21 Fitting
24 Christmas carols
25 "You didn't have to tell me"
26 Plants with needles
27 Dead duck
28 "___ next time!"
29 Director Kurosawa
30 Li'l ___
31 Sauce, cheese or noodles, in lasagna
32 Gladiatorial combat site
37 Examine, as a crystal ball
38 Gradually slowing, in music
41 High achievers?
43 Pizza company with a game piece logo
45 Summer setting in D.C.
46 Spreadsheet figures

49 Island instruments, for short
50 Website with the heading "Recently Viewed Items"
51 Style of the Chrysler Building, informally
52 It gets hit on the head
53 Eye amorously
54 Ruhr refusal
55 Opening on a schedule
56 Precursor of Diet Coke
57 Director DuVernay of "Selma"

by Zachary Spitz and Diane Roseman

ACROSS

1 Dict. entries
4 Spinner in a PC drive
9 H.S. class for a future doctor, maybe
14 Good name for a tax adviser?
15 In the know
16 Sound from a hen
17 Big name in athletic wear
19 Underworld, in Greek mythology
20 Mean dog, at times
21 Pines (for)
22 Gumbo vegetable
23 Jellystone Park toon with a bow tie
27 "Girlfriend" boy band
29 ___ personality (Dr. Jekyll and Mr. Hyde trait)
30 Bill with Jefferson's portrait
31 Siri runs on it
33 Sac fly result
34 Breather
35 Assortment of appetizers at a Polynesian or Chinese restaurant
38 Stiffly formal
40 Stephen of "The Crying Game"
41 Be under the weather
42 Particle accelerator particle
43 Flight deck guesses about takeoff, for short
45 Loses color
49 Amorous look
53 Bread dipped in hummus
54 Winter neckwear
55 Court jesters, e.g.
57 Set of moral principles
58 Noisemakers at the 2010 World Cup
60 Letter after gamma
61 Former "Saturday Night Live" regular Cheri
62 Horatian creation
63 Gown
64 Some squishy balls
65 Marry

DOWN

1 President during W.W. I
2 Boozehounds
3 $400,000/year, for the U.S. president
4 Telephone
5 Social misfit
6 Implement for a muzzleloader
7 Acapulco gold
8 Three Wise ___ (Magi)
9 Sneezing sound
10 Backup strategy
11 Person in charge of fiscal decisions
12 Arctic fishing tools
13 Approvals
18 Radioactive element
21 Novel narrated by Humbert Humbert
24 Title for the Virgin Mary
25 ___ ghanouj
26 Decompose
28 Beat patroller
32 Having no doubt about
34 Medical setback
35 Game played with a 48-card deck
36 Tennis great Sampras
37 Gratuity
38 Bacon source
39 One sounding "cock-a-doodle-doo"
44 Pitcher Tom nicknamed "The Franchise"
46 Keep out of sight
47 Investment company whose commercials once had talking babies
48 Mouthed off to
50 Manners of walking
51 Killer whales
52 Blue toon whose enemy is Gargamel
56 Commando weapons
57 TV announcer Hall whose credits include "The Tonight Show"
58 Germany's Otto ___ Bismarck
59 Sport-___ (rugged vehicle)

by Peter Gordon

ACROSS

1 Matches, as a bet
5 Suffix with bachelor
9 Miss
13 Pinball game ender
14 Keisters
16 Mozart's "Se vuol ballare," for one
17 Neck of the woods
18 Very, in music
19 "Darn it all!"
20 Practical sort . . . or anagram #1 of the only seven letters used to make this puzzle
22 Ballpark gates
24 Times when the French go en vacances
25 Chasing Moby Dick, say
26 Brightest 1-Down in Aquila
29 Big celeb . . . or anagram #2
32 Bollywood wraps
33 Formal ceremonies
34 One of a pair of map coordinates: Abbr.
36 Awaken
37 Tennis great Monica
38 Meter maid of song
39 Asian new year
40 Animals rounded up in a roundup
41 Foodie, e.g.
42 Sells (for) . . . or anagram #3
44 Standing still
45 The black square chunk in front of 55-, 60- and 63-Across, and others
46 Actor Morales
47 Zionist's homeland
50 More coarse . . . or anagram #4
54 Social reformer Jacob
55 Californie and others
58 "Dies ___"
59 Vogue rival
60 U. S. Grant rival
61 "He'd fly through the air with the greatest of ___" (old song lyric)
62 Suffix with prank or poll
63 "___ we forget . . ."
64 Concordes, for short

DOWN

1 Sky light
2 Blarney Stone land
3 Zeno's home
4 Result of poor ventilation
5 Pink Pearl, for one
6 Things graded by 7-Down
7 See 6-Down
8 1970s political cause, for short
9 It may be thrown from a horse
10 ___ Sea (former fourth-largest lake in the world)
11 Babylon, for the ancient Hanging Gardens
12 Lip
15 Fraidy-cats
21 "That so?"
23 Thomas Hardy heroine
25 Take up or let out
26 Admin. aide
27 "See ya"
28 Like the invitation line "Be there or be square"
29 Roger formerly of Fox News
30 Crème de la crème
31 Deserves V.I.P. treatment
33 Predigital film units
35 Piquant
37 Ben of "Tower Heist"
38 They come along once in a blue moon
40 Store window sign
41 List-ending abbr.
43 Come-on
44 How tableware is often sold
46 ___ Park, Colo.
47 Seriously vexes
48 Delta deposit
49 Vex
51 Nest eggs for the golden yrs.
52 Big ___ Conference
53 Roger who played a part on "Cheers"
56 Certain util. bill
57 Stein filler

by Bruce Haight

ACROSS

1 Web designer's code
5 One wearing an apron and a puffy white hat
9 One includes "My cup runneth over" in the Bible
14 Has debts
15 Slight amount
16 Like a wolf's howl in the dead of night
17 Gobbledygook
19 Looked open-mouthed
20 Scot's cap
21 "___ is me!"
22 Up in arms
24 Nebraska's capital before Lincoln
26 Grandson of Adam
27 Clock-setting std.
30 Big fat zero
34 Like Jefferson on a list of presidents
35 River through Paris
36 Do laps in a pool
39 Flower that's also a girl's name
42 Spoonful of medicine, say
43 Put forward, as an idea
45 Unlocks
47 Habitual tube watchers
51 Swiss peak
52 Part in a movie
53 Hair that hangs over the forehead
56 Used a lever on
58 "Golly!"
60 Promise-to-pay note
61 Capital of South Korea
63 What a shamed person has to "eat"
66 Stand on three legs?
67 Mideast native
68 On the ___ (recuperating)
69 Lock of hair
70 Metal canisters
71 Hankering

DOWN

1 Book consulted by a do-it-yourselfer
2 Time in Manhattan when it's midnight in Montana
3 Ethel who sang "There's No Business Like Show Business"
4 It was often dropped in the '60s
5 "See ya!"
6 Woodchuck's escape route
7 Airline app datum, for short
8 On the decline
9 Flying horse of Greek myth
10 "Save me a ___!"
11 Notes of a chord played in rapid succession
12 Fib
13 Club ___
18 Path of mowed grass
23 Steal from
25 It might capture an embarrassing comment
26 Bit of appended text
28 Store department selling suits and ties
29 Obstacle for a drone
31 Modern and cool
32 Plan that might include mutual funds, in brief
33 Body of water that separates Africa and Asia
36 Pet safety org.
37 Sheep's coat
38 "It's certainly possible . . ."
40 Hot spring
41 "The best is ___ to come"
44 What amusement parks provide
46 2016 prize for Bob Dylan
48 Who wrote of "sorrow for the lost Lenore"
49 Out-of-date
50 Marksman with an M40
54 Word cried twice before "gone"
55 Napped leather
57 Feels remorse over
58 F.B.I. worker, informally
59 Recedes
61 Ready
62 Place for a bud or a stud
64 Celebrity psychic Geller
65 Down Under bird

by Gary Cee

ACROSS

1 Country invaded in 2003
5 H.S. math class
9 Legendary music club in Lower Manhattan, informally
14 Suffix with refresh or replace
15 Parks of Alabama
16 Spartan serf
17 *V.I.P.'s security agent
19 Resort island near Majorca
20 The Rams of the Atlantic 10 Conf.
21 Scholarship money
22 *Nintendo hand-held
24 Disgorges
26 Actress Campbell of "Scream"
27 *Place to plug in a USB cable
33 "Ditto"
36 Utters, informally
37 Does the honors for Thanksgiving dinner
38 Short-sheeting, e.g.
40 Snoring sound
42 Tuscan city
43 Sees eye to eye (with)
45 52, in old Rome
47 Long, single take, in filmmaking
48 *Multiplex, e.g.
51 Stew morsels
52 Exchange vows at the altar
56 *NATO's smallest member, populationwise
60 Stock listings: Abbr.
61 Ariz. neighbor
62 Sacha Baron Cohen character
63 *Where a newspaper's biggest stories go
66 Actress Gaynor of "South Pacific"
67 "E pluribus ___"

68 "So ___ walks into . . ."
69 Fall of winter
70 What a ponytail partially covers
71 There's no place like it . . . or a word that can precede either half of the answer to each starred clue

DOWN

1 Fill (with)
2 Corporate shuffle, for short
3 Love interest of Pacey on "Dawson's Creek"
4 Amt.
5 "What's right is right" and others
6 Rocky ___
7 Haifa's country: Abbr.
8 Doohickey

9 Monstrous creatures
10 French newborn
11 Smooth-talking
12 Schmo
13 "___ With Me" (Sam Smith hit)
18 Purrer in Peru
23 Opposite of sans
25 Act starter
26 Shows some affection
28 Dispenser candy
29 Religious abode
30 Baker's need
31 Artist Magritte
32 Romanov ruler
33 Often-filtered messages
34 Jason's ship
35 ___ Levy, Buffalo Bills coach in the Hall of Fame
39 "Don't quit!"

41 1980s Pakistani president
44 W.W. II-era British gun
46 Treater's phrase
49 Enjoyed oneself
50 Wind tile in mah-jongg
53 Insect stage
54 Use Goo Gone on, perhaps
55 Daisy variety
56 Some old PCs
57 Snake's shape
58 Art Deco notable
59 Loaf (around)
60 Government overthrow
64 Single-stranded molecule
65 Part of a tuba's sound

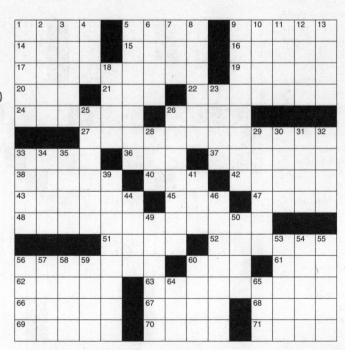

by Gary J. Whitehead

ACROSS

1 Bouts, as of crying
5 ___ Le Pew (cartoon skunk)
9 Fizzy headache remedy, informally
14 Bra size smaller than a "B"
15 Highway sign next to an off-ramp
16 Extend, as a subscription
17 Not giving up on an argument, say
19 Throat-clearing sounds
20 Words attributed to 41-Across
22 Wyatt of the Old West
23 Hi-___ monitor
24 Apt cry for 41-Across
31 Moving day rental
32 Big laughs, slangily
33 Symbol of busyness
34 Cosmologist Sagan
35 Ninnies
37 Parsley, sage, rosemary or thyme
38 Fleur-de-___
39 Money that needs to be repaid
40 Dresses in Delhi
41 Famous queen, depicted literally
45 Early Beatle ___ Sutcliffe
46 Put into piles, say
47 Something committed by 41-Across . . . or by this puzzle's creator?
54 Attend a funeral, say
55 Merchandise location
56 Keepsake in a cabinet, perhaps
57 Competitor of Wisk
58 First among men
59 Minor fights
60 Cards sometimes hidden up sleeves
61 Blood components

DOWN

1 Monopoly space with the words "Just Visiting"
2 Pimples
3 Wind that might blow one's hat off
4 Malicious
5 Czar called "the Great"
6 Not taxable, e.g.
7 Wood for many a mountain cabin
8 Grammy-winning James
9 Pick-me-up drinks
10 It's nothing new
11 Short race spec
12 Bit of viral web content
13 Cries of pain
18 Article thrown over the shoulders
21 Long, hard journeys
24 Atheist Madalyn Murray ___
25 Persian tongue
26 Prefix relating to sleep
27 Shade of color
28 Fellow film critic of Siskel
29 Eagle's home
30 Belles of the ball
31 The Bruins of the Pac-12
35 Krispy Kreme product
36 Grain used in making Alpha-Bits
37 North Carolina's Cape ___
39 Many Americans whose names end in -ez
40 Feudal workers
42 ___ de corps (fellowship)
43 Tristan's beloved
44 Certain bank policy for A.T.M. withdrawals and wire transfers
47 Brilliant move
48 Ambient quality
49 "The Thin Man" canine
50 Of the flock
51 Point where lines meet
52 Fly high
53 Jane Austen heroine
54 Roast hosts, for short

by Ed Sessa

ACROSS

1 Like some basketball shots and unwanted calls
8 Slangy turndown
11 Law man
14 Woo
15 ___ crossroads
16 ". . . fish ___ fowl"
17 Markswoman dubbed "Little Sure Shot" [1977]
19 Male swan
20 Site of two French banks
21 Free from
22 Prefix with center
23 High lines
25 Variety of pool [1982]
27 2017 N.C.A.A. basketball champs
30 Opposite of a gulp
32 Rapidly spreading over the internet
33 Mushroom or balloon
35 Group that takes pledges, informally
38 Massage target?
39 Capital city with only about 1,000 residents [2016]
44 Stew morsel
45 "Right away!"
46 Geraint's wife, in Arthurian legend
47 Understand
49 Rallying cry?
51 "Gloria in Excelsis ___" (hymn)
52 Landlord's register [1996]
56 Ring on a string
58 Columbia, for one
59 Winds down in a pit?
61 Boise's home
65 President pro ___
66 Award won by the starts of 17-, 25-, 39- and 52-Across and 11- and 29-Down

68 ___-la-la
69 Get a good look at
70 Country north of Latvia
71 Hankering
72 70-Across, e.g., formerly: Abbr.
73 TV's "Maverick" or "Gunsmoke"

DOWN

1 They may be strapless or padded
2 Solo
3 Luxury hotel chain
4 Oscar winner for "Hannah and Her Sisters"
5 Prepares to be knighted
6 Prefix with tourism
7 Sweetie
8 Nita of silent films
9 Used as the surface for a meal
10 Antihistamine target
11 400 meters, for an Olympic track [2012]
12 Commotion
13 Clay character in old "S.N.L." sketches
18 They're related
24 Search (through)
26 1996 Foo Fighters hit
27 "That's awful!"
28 Hunters' org.
29 Superloyal employee [1971]
31 Crackerjacks
34 Oscar winner for "Hannah and Her Sisters"
36 Caste member
37 Means of avoiding an uphill climb

40 Blankets for open-air travelers
41 Series ender: Abbr.
42 Run out of power
43 Commotion
47 Courageously persistent
48 Noted colonial silversmith
50 Bank jobs
53 Follows orders
54 Deadbeat, e.g.
55 Tennis call
57 Buffoon
60 Eurasian duck
62 Teen woe
63 Wig, e.g.
64 Pearl Buck heroine
67 Helpfulness

by David J. Kahn

ACROSS

1 4.0 is a great one
4 Nearsighted cartoon Mr.
9 Garbage-carrying boats
14 Superannuated
15 Denim or linen
16 Ancient land near Lydia
17 Not good
18 "Super 8" actress, 2011
20 Relative who might visit for the holidays
22 Hightail it
23 Secret language
24 "Thanks, Captain Obvious!"
27 Ltr. addition
28 One-named New Age singer
29 Rough, as criticism
31 Industrious little marchers
34 Spring school dance
37 How sardines are often packed
39 "Get the picture?"
40 Flower that attracts pollinating insects
42 Actress Thurman
43 Money in the middle of a poker table
45 Farm tower
46 High point
47 Auto deal for nonbuyers
49 Caltech, e.g.: Abbr.
51 Talk, talk and then talk some more
52 Whistlers in the kitchen
58 Brief letter
59 Dr. Mom's attention, for short
60 Each one in a square is 90°
61 Order to get a soundtrack ready
65 Popular pen
66 Money in the middle of a poker table

67 ___ raving mad
68 Toddler
69 Deal negotiator for athletes
70 State where the Cotton Bowl is held
71 There are four in a gallon: Abbr.

DOWN

1 Not hold back
2 Air Force One, for one
3 Bewilder
4 Ian who wrote "Atonement"
5 Every last bit
6 Fútbol score
7 Onetime "S.N.L." regular Cheri
8 "That sounds good . . . NOT!"
9 Envy or lust
10 Worry

11 Dish in a bowl often served au gratin
12 Tinkler on a porch
13 Wise man
19 Egyptian cross
21 Thumbs-up votes
25 Variety
26 Relatives of rabbits
30 "We ___ to please!"
31 Word before "and ye shall receive"
32 Singer with the 1972 hit "Heart of Gold"
33 One-on-one talk
35 Sash for a kimono
36 Pop singer Zayn formerly of One Direction
38 Opposite of strict
40 Fly-___ (Blue Angels maneuvers)
41 Lacking company
44 Rest for a bit

46 Abbr. before a name on a memo
48 Suffix with cigar
50 Groups of poker chips, typically
53 Locale of a film "nightmare": Abbr.
54 Less than 90°
55 Modern movement initialism . . . or a hint to the starts of 18-, 24-, 40-, 52- and 61-Across
56 "The Waste Land" poet
57 Religious offshoots
58 March Madness org.
62 President before D.D.E.
63 Jazz instrument
64 Savings for the golden years, for short

by Zhouqin Burnikel

ACROSS

1 Social adroitness
5 City between Gainesville and Orlando
10 Skateboarder's incline
14 Radar response
15 Mushroom variety
16 Garfield's foil in the comics
17 View furtively
19 Main role
20 Direct, as a collision
21 John of "Saturday Night Fever"
23 Amber Alert, e.g., for short
24 Complete the negotiations
25 Like the number of games in a "best of" series
27 Cut (off)
29 Pitchfork point
30 Secure some urban transportation
33 Rejoice
37 Oscar winner Jared of "Dallas Buyers Club"
38 Buy and sell, as stocks
41 Jacob's biblical twin
42 Decorative pitchers
44 Was vaccinated
46 Pinch in the kitchen
49 Hit with a Taser
50 Terre Haute sch.
51 Prepare for someone's birthday, perhaps
55 Org. for top-notch H.S. students
57 Blue-blooded
58 Hollywood's Diane, Buster or Michael
61 Seed cover
62 Briefly put pen to paper, say
64 "Don't touch that, honey!"
65 Engine capacity unit
66 Increase
67 Poses a poser
68 Relatively cool red giant
69 The second "S" of MS-DOS: Abbr.

DOWN

1 Radio host John
2 Teenage skin malady
3 Takeout food together with a Netflix movie, maybe
4 Garden amphibians
5 Tip of the Arabian Peninsula
6 "Brooklyn Nine-Nine" figure
7 Rocky glacial ridge
8 Look upon with lust
9 High-pH substance
10 Obsolescent desktop accessories
11 "Hello" singer, 2015
12 Sporty Mazda
13 Organ part
18 Qantas Airways symbol
22 Barn topper
24 Practice boxing
25 Look upon with lust
26 Was the clue giver in Pictionary
28 Start of the fourth qtr.
31 Brothels
32 Give up on, in slang
34 Class that covers Reconstruction and Prohibition
35 Neighbor of Vietnam
36 "Swan Lake" article of attire
39 Nod off
40 Letter between zeta and theta
43 Swedish aircraft giant
45 Breathing problem
47 Frowny looks
48 ___ tweed
51 Swahili master
52 Nestlé bars filled with tiny bubbles
53 "Hogan's Heroes" colonel
54 Noted berry farm founder Walter
56 Puts up, as a painting
58 Deborah of "The King and I"
59 Plains tribe members
60 Politico Gingrich
63 Drink with crumpets

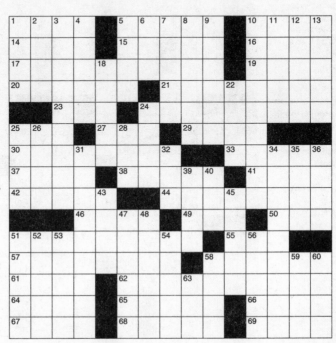

by Peter A. Collins

ACROSS

1 Fruit often seen in still lifes
5 Black wood
10 Fable's message
15 Opera highlight
16 Elaine's last name on "Seinfeld"
17 Flabbergast
18 Historic California route, with "El"
20 Schmoozing gossip
21 Bottoms of high-tops
22 Departs
23 Desirable feature of a rented room
29 Mathematician Turing who was the subject of "The Imitation Game"
30 Genetic copies
31 Forwards, as a misdelivered letter
35 Weaving machine
36 Mani-pedi place
39 2016 film for which Viggo Mortensen earned an Oscar nomination
42 Pig's digs
43 Ancient France
44 Navigation instrument
45 Many Monty Python skits
47 Crumb carriers
48 Common computer peripherals
54 Sigher's words
55 College officials
56 "Here's to the newlyweds!," e.g.
58 Part of a person's psyche . . . or a hidden part of 18-, 23-, 39- or 48-Across?
63 Wonderland girl
64 Division of a play
65 Notion
66 Chill out
67 Played (with)
68 Polo mount

DOWN

1 "Super" group buying campaign ads
2 One-third of pitching's Triple Crown, for short
3 Command between "Ready!" and "Fire!"
4 Chocolate-covered morsel often eaten at the movies
5 Virus in 2014 news
6 Special Forces cap
7 "Gimme a minute"
8 Schoolteacher's org.
9 French designer's monogram
10 With 62-Down, a spring festival
11 Symbols of resistance
12 Talked incessantly
13 Quetzalcoatl worshiper
14 Car deal that's not a purchase
19 Election mo.
23 Skirt fold
24 Hoarse
25 "___ Enchanted" (2004 film)
26 "High" times
27 Govt.-issued security
28 Century 21 rival
29 Paths of pendulums
32 Bother persistently
33 Book with handwritten thoughts
34 Ducked (out) furtively
36 Easel, e.g.
37 Pub purchases
38 Divisions of a play
40 Escape
41 The Enterprise, for example
45 Soft drink in a green bottle
46 2000 Summer Olympics city
48 Smallest OPEC nation
49 Entire
50 Letter that doesn't need an envelope or stamp
51 Designer Geoffrey
52 Got into a row?
53 Nelson Mandela's org.
57 ___-Mex
58 "Was ___ das?" (German question)
59 Cpl., e.g.
60 Altar affirmation
61 Spy novelist Deighton
62 See 10-Down

by Peter Gordon

ACROSS

1 Whole slew
5 Outer protein shell of a virus
11 Verve
14 "Celeste Aida," e.g.
15 Futures analyst?
16 Famous Tokyo-born singer
17 WASHINGTON + R = Intimidation tactic
19 Option words
20 Fusions
21 Smoked marijuana
23 Word repeated in "Ring Around the Rosy" before "We all fall down"
24 MISSOURI + E = "No fooling!"
26 Interpret
27 Martin who wrote "London Fields"
28 Short dance wear
29 Rode the bench
30 Whopper inventor
31 Marching well
33 MARYLAND + O = Period in which nothing special happens
35 Imps are little ones
38 Sacagawea dollar, e.g.
39 ___-relief
42 Evelyn Waugh's writer brother
43 Laborious task
44 Salad green
45 NEBRASKA + T = Mortgage specifications
48 Aid for administering an oath of office
49 Segment of a binge-watch
50 Prince William's mom
51 Mule's father
52 CALIFORNIA + N = Majestic beast
55 1920s car

56 Parodied
57 "___ it ironic?"
58 Phishing target: Abbr.
59 Gave an exam
60 "Divergent" actor James

DOWN

1 Places where oysters are served
2 Victim of river diversion in Asia
3 Professional headgear that's stereotypically red
4 Got some sun
5 Fleeces
6 S. Amer. home of the tango
7 Ballet step
8 Straight downhill run on skis

9 "You win," alternatively
10 Put off
11 Get dog-tired
12 Neither here nor there?
13 Prepares to shoot near the basket, say
18 Phishing targets, briefly
22 Scatterbrained
24 Muslim leader
25 One-in-a-million event
27 Affected manner
30 [You crack me up]
31 "Understood, dude"
32 A Bobbsey twin
33 Shaving mishaps
34 English johns
35 Chicago squad in old "S.N.L." skits
36 Passes by

37 Hunter's freezerful, maybe
39 Infantile
40 "Finished!"
41 View, as the future
43 Rears of ships
44 "Curious George" books, e.g.
46 Honor with insults
47 Charge for a plug?
48 Complete block
50 SoCal force
53 Big inits. in the aerospace industry
54 Nod from offstage, maybe

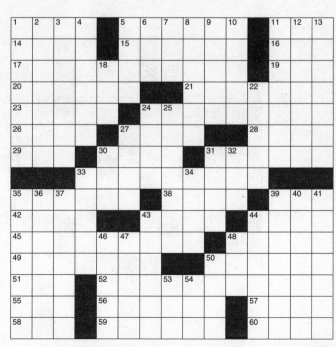

by Bruce Haight

ACROSS

1 With 43- and 76-Across, camping aid
6 1950s prez
9 Place to play the slots
15 Veranda
16 They're "Red" in Boston and "White" in Chicago
17 Third-party account
18 "S.N.L." alum Cheri
19 Homie
20 Heroin or Vicodin
21 One function of 1-/43-/76-Across
23 Double curves, as on highways
24 Mournful bell sounds
25 Nuts for squirrels
28 Chop (off)
29 Greek goddess of victory
30 Not fooled by
34 "___ before beauty"
37 Insect in a colony
39 Maple syrup source
40 "Purple ___" (Prince hit)
41 Medicare drug benefit
43 See 1-Across
45 Band that made Justin Timberlake famous
46 Cole ___ (side dish)
47 "___-la-la"
48 Sign of a sellout
50 Sault ___ Marie, Mich.
51 Otherwise
52 Org. advocating pet adoption
54 Like baseball's Pacific Coast League
56 Removed, as chalk
58 Resurrection figure
62 Fad
65 One function of 1-/43-/76-Across
67 "I'd be delighted"
69 12 months, in Tijuana
70 Pong game maker

71 Chef Lagasse
72 ___ de Janeiro
73 Arrested
74 Came clean, with "up"
75 Concorde, for short
76 See 1-Across

DOWN

1 "Mr." on the Enterprise
2 King of the gods in Wagner's "Ring" cycle
3 Memorable 2011 hurricane
4 Form of a papyrus document
5 All a tanker can hold
6 Library ID
7 Cuisine with kimchi
8 Casting out of a demon
9 Corp. head
10 "Quaking" tree
11 One function of 1-/43-/76-Across
12 Nest eggs for later years, in brief
13 Do, re or mi
14 Is in debt
22 Home of "Monday Night Football"
26 Gives the go-ahead
27 Agent, in brief
31 "No" votes
32 Windshield feature
33 Fairy tale's first word
34 Altar area
35 Chutzpah
36 Historical periods
38 Coverings pulled across infields
42 One function of 1-/43-/76-Across
44 Indy vehicles
45 Refuge during the Great Flood

47 Airport screening org.
49 Pool table triangle
53 Handsome man
55 Inverse trig function
57 Fix, as a knot
59 Tehran native
60 Feature lacked by Helvetica type
61 Bale binder
62 Word after bass or treble
63 Where all roads lead, it's said
64 Madison and Fifth in Manhattan: Abbr.
66 Word sung three times before "for the home team" in "Take Me Out to the Ball Game"
68 Not new

by Gary Kennedy

ACROSS

1 Make a pass at
6 Cousin of lager
9 Deposited soil
13 Dig deeply
14 Baldwin known for his presidential impersonation
15 Village Voice award
16 Dress down
18 TD Garden athlete, informally
19 Gorge oneself, with "out"
20 Smidgen
21 Salmon type
23 Wash. neighbor
24 San ___, Italy
26 "Live Free or Die Hard" director Wiseman
27 Potentially offensive
30 Bread that's often brushed with ghee
31 Early anesthetic
34 Main line from the heart
36 Aquafina competitor
37 "Wow, unbelievable!"
40 Cause of yawns
41 Kitchen cabinet
42 Rainbow ___
43 Others, in Oaxaca
44 "A Dream Within a Dream" writer
45 Big college major, informally
49 Suffix with morph-
50 Onetime giant in consumer electronics
52 Fair-hiring letters
53 Audited, as a class
56 "Be quiet!"
58 X-ray alternative
59 Coveted, as a position
60 Throws a fit
63 Fairy tale meanie
64 Marriott competitor
65 Core belief
66 Lies by the pool, say
67 Penn of "Harold & Kumar" films
68 Figure skating event . . . or what the circled items always come in

DOWN

1 Quaint fashion accessory
2 Enthusiastic assent
3 Friendly Islands native
4 www.wikipedia.___
5 Neither fem. nor masc.
6 Pie ___ mode
7 Future perfect tense in grammar class, e.g.
8 Bounce back
9 Some mechanics' tool collections
10 Informal cry from someone who is duped
11 Bloom on a pad
12 Part lopped off by la guillotine
14 How pasta may be prepared
17 Talent for music
22 Fully explain
25 Nanny goat's cry
28 Plays charades
29 Make rough
32 Brian who composed "Discreet Music"
33 What an air ball misses
35 Train system: Abbr.
36 Scooby-___
37 Big step for a young company, for short
38 Silent "Welcome" giver
39 Reciprocally
40 Cold one
42 You, in Tours
44 Isthmus land
46 Native of Mocha
47 Drugstore location, often
48 Bank jobs
51 Sashimi staple
53 Dalmatian feature
54 Pond organism
55 "Well, all right then"
57 Start of a web address
61 TV show that comes on at 11:29 (not 11:30) p.m.
62 Pekoe, for one

by Zhouqin Burnikel

ACROSS

1 TV network whose logo is an eye
4 Singer Mitchell who wrote "Woodstock" (but didn't attend)
8 Whole
14 The "A" of I.P.A.
15 Former Israeli P.M. Ehud
16 ___ Tunes (Warner Bros. cartoons)
17 Epoch of rare distinction
19 Tool for the Grim Reaper
20 Opposites of true believers
21 Optima and Cadenza car company
22 "If only ___ listened . . ."
23 Archie's wife on "All in the Family"
24 Topic of a happy annual report
27 ___ Pieces
29 Celestial Seasonings product
30 Greet with humility
31 Jul. follower
33 Dow Jones stat.
35 Shocked response
36 Something circled on a calendar
40 Second-largest Hawaiian island
42 Aperitif with black currant liqueur
43 ___ Paulo, Brazil
44 Darkest part of a shadow
46 Bro, e.g.
48 Concepts not meant to be questioned
53 Period of supreme courage and achievement
56 One-named rap star
57 To and ___
58 Fact-gathering org.
59 Do a perfunctory performance
61 Substituted "math" for "mass," say

63 When TV viewership peaks . . . or a hint to 17-, 24-, 36- and 53-Across
64 Timeless, to Shakespeare
65 Houses in Havana
66 TV network whose logo is a peacock
67 Puts back to 0, say
68 X-ray ___ (gag gift)
69 "We all ___ little mad sometimes": Norman Bates

DOWN

1 More evasive with the truth
2 Marilyn Monroe, notably
3 Something you reach out and take?
4 Author Austen
5 Toothbrush brand
6 Bothers the conscience of
7 Eisenhower, informally
8 Borden milk mascot
9 Like a diet lacking bread or pasta, for short
10 Etch A Sketch or yo-yo
11 Blocking someone's path
12 Puts back in the oven
13 Visine application
15 Tousled look of the recently woken
18 Counterparts of dahs in Morse code
21 Scoundrels
25 In apple-pie order
26 Mind-body exercise
28 Sit and mope
32 Performer with a fan
34 One finally done with finals?
36 Kiss like an Eskimo
37 Land of Blarney
38 Duo plus one
39 Idle drawings

40 Part of a car's exhaust system
41 "You agree with me?," informally
45 Goal for a mountaineer
47 Trumped-up charge
49 Fortitude
50 Beating at chess
51 With hands on hips
52 ___ Falls, N.Y.
54 Neap and ebb
55 Uplift
60 Big movie format
62 ___-K (early schooling)
63 Mac alternatives

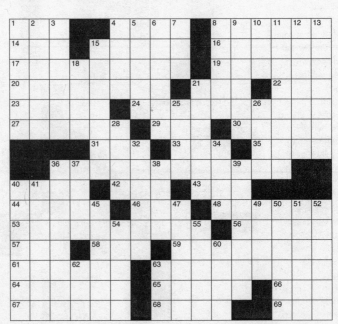

by Jeff Chen and Seth Geltman

ACROSS

1 Peruvian of long ago
5 The end
10 Simoleon
14 Bend to one side
15 "Don't Cry for Me Argentina" musical
16 Where Nepal is
17 Horse breed known for dressage [western writer]
19 Rogen of "Neighbors"
20 It helps you see plays in replays
21 "Finding Dory" fish
22 Genesis garden
23 Raggedy ___
25 Bolt go-with
27 Upset stomach remedy [Brontë governess]
35 Catholic service
36 Dropped a bit
37 Sluggish
38 Modern bookmark
39 Like a silhouette [19th-century U.K. prime minister]
41 Chrysler truck
42 Surface for chalk writing
44 Intend
45 Fortitude
46 Really made the point [TV surgeon played by Ellen Pompeo]
49 Praising poem
50 Pronoun for two or more
51 Tell all
54 "My goodness!"
58 Sprang
62 Its logo consists of four interlocking circles
63 Brains . . . or this puzzle's four shaded names?
65 Public transit option
66 "Storage Wars" network
67 Abate
68 Beach hill
69 One starting a story "Back in my day . . . ," say
70 ___ 360 (game console)

DOWN

1 Pains
2 Justice Gorsuch
3 Guitarist's key-changing aid
4 Zoo collection
5 Tasseled Turkish topper
6 Boxer Drago of "Rocky IV"
7 Highest figure in sudoku
8 List component
9 Island wrap
10 The decimal system
11 Took advantage of
12 Reference
13 Madeline of "Blazing Saddles"
18 Prize you don't want on "Let's Make a Deal"
24 Wine quality
26 Collection of textbook chapters
27 An ex of Donald Trump
28 Religion with the Five Pillars
29 Olympic symbol
30 Bogged down
31 Dwight's opponent in 1952 and '56
32 Liquid hospital supply
33 Furious
34 20 dispensers
35 "Let's go!" to sled dogs
39 Clarinet piece
40 Sondheim's "___ the Woods"
43 Sprint competitor
45 Waterproof fabric
47 Ska relative
48 Dance at a 52-Down
51 Shakespeare, for one
52 Event with 48-Down dancing
53 Pre-service announcement?
55 ___ exam
56 Text message button
57 One side of a Stevenson character
59 Open ___ (start at the bar, maybe)
60 Mexican moolah
61 Fearsome dino
64 Debussy's sea

by Neville Fogarty

ACROSS

1 Doofus
5 Campus bigwig
9 Leave standing at the altar
13 Greek counterpart to Mars
14 "Tickle Me" doll
15 Walks in water up to one's ankles, say
16 Early radio transmitter
18 Download for a Kindle
19 Deep-frying need
20 "The Farmer in the ___"
22 Letter after "ar"
23 Apply gently, as cream
25 Part of "business," phonetically
30 "Raiders of the Lost Ark" star
32 102, in ancient Rome
34 Common Market letters
35 A sensible sort
36 Like a sorry-looking dog
38 Tiny
40 Very thin, as clouds
41 How some ground balls are fielded
43 Longtime news inits.
45 "___ whillikers!"
46 One-cent coin since 1909
49 Ballet footwear
50 Email address ending for a student
51 Busy bee in Apr.
54 Oil cartel
56 Useful item for finding a lost pet
58 Brief brawl
62 Common game in a school gym
64 Soothing succulents
65 U2's lead singer
66 Biblical brother with a birthright
67 Bad thing to blow . . . or what each of the circled letters in this puzzle represents
68 Greek H's
69 Some whistle blowers

DOWN

1 Wash oneself
2 Stackable cookies
3 Citrus peels
4 Norway's capital
5 Announce
6 "Xanadu" band, for short
7 In the thick of
8 At least
9 The "one" in a one-two
10 Vow from a bride or groom
11 Sign between Cancer and Virgo
12 "Shame on you!"
15 "Ver-r-ry interesting!"
17 Elton John/Tim Rice Broadway musical
21 11-Down symbol
24 Prepare, as tea
26 Dummy at a protest march
27 Lasso loop
28 Figure of speech
29 Without purpose
30 Hard-to-hit pitches
31 Freeze
32 Tragic clown in "Pagliacci"
33 Lacking sense
36 Shed old feathers
37 Casual calls
39 Blade in a sporting match
42 Alka-Seltzer sound
44 Blue hues
47 As required, after "if"
48 Classic art subject
51 Pursue, as in tag
52 Rice dish
53 Highest possible grade
55 Geezer
57 Trucker on a radio
58 Never left the bench, say
59 Inventor Whitney
60 Craggy peak
61 Letter after 22-Across
63 Paternity identifier

by Paul Coulter

ACROSS

1 Inner parts of corn
5 Nectar source
10 Turn toward
14 "The ___ King"
15 Hayfield worker
16 Airline that flies only six days a week
17 Jessica of filmdom's "Fantastic Four"
18 Duck for cover?
19 Toy block brand
20 Regulation regarding a 2007 #1 Rihanna hit?
23 Jazzy Reese
24 Bagel topper
25 Dallas-to-N.Y.C. direction
26 Jamaican spirits
29 Letters on an N.Y.C.-bound bag
30 Friend's opposite
33 Special observances for a 2014 #1 Pharrell Williams hit?
37 "Damn right!"
39 Cry before "set, go!"
40 Tick off
41 1994 #1 Lisa Loeb hit played at a potluck?
44 Where one might chill
45 The Shangri-___ ("Leader of the Pack" group)
46 Em chasers
47 ___-friendly
50 The "O" of S O S, apocryphally
51 Important exam
53 1979 #1 Styx hit played for Little Red Riding Hood?
59 Go out for a while?
60 ___ and aahed
61 Sass, in slang
62 Israeli arms
63 Course reversal
64 Feudin' with
65 Radiate, as charm
66 Hit home?
67 Females

DOWN

1 Composer Debussy
2 Some Texas tycoons
3 Toy in a souvenir shop
4 Problem for a comb
5 Adam's family member
6 Olympic track gold medalist Devers
7 "M*A*S*H" man
8 Hit HBO show for Julia Louis-Dreyfus
9 Swashbuckling leading man
10 ___ the Cat
11 Trump impersonator Baldwin
12 Hard to fool
13 "Do Ya" rock grp.
21 Wyatt of the Old West
22 Mythical mischief-maker
27 Really funny
28 Mike who played filmdom's Austin Powers
29 Foster child in "Freaky Friday"
30 "Point taken"
31 Olive of cartoons
32 Japan finish?
34 At ___ rate
35 "You ___ me at 'hello' "
36 Dr. who can't write prescriptions
37 Nile menace
38 N.Y.C. subway overseer
42 Chimney vent
43 Warning letters next to a web link
48 Club attendant
49 Twins Mary-Kate and Ashley
50 Jabba-esque
52 Smidgens
53 Classic TV clown
54 Comic Ansari
55 "The Little Red Hen" refusal
56 Heavy-landing sound
57 Not yonder
58 Bespectacled Dame of comedy
59 Hall & Oates, for example

by Lisa Loeb and Doug Peterson

ACROSS

1 Skilled
6 What's more
10 "Once ___ a time . . ."
14 "___ got a deal for you!"
15 Apply, as plaster
16 Repellent
17 First of a series of sci-fi movies starring Sigourney Weaver
18 10:1, for example
19 Computer command for the error-prone
20 Actor who has hosted the Oscars nine times, a number second only to Bob Hope
23 Something stubbed
24 Powerful explosive
28 Baseball's ___ Joe DiMaggio
32 Watchdog org.?
34 Wrath
35 Sound of danger
36 He played Gomez in 1991's "The Addams Family"
38 Prefix with -zoic
39 Tube-shaped pasta
40 Geese formations
41 Comic actor who was an original cast member of SCTV
43 Swiss capital, to French speakers
44 India pale ___
45 Affectedly creative
46 Wild animals
47 Club Med, for one
49 The "f" of fwiw
50 Beginning of a rom-com . . . or a description of 20-, 36- and 41-Across?
57 In fine fettle
60 College in New Rochelle, N.Y.
61 Bert's pal on "Sesame Street"
62 Word of woe

63 Thumbs-down votes
64 Repeated short bits in jazz
65 Agree (with)
66 Itsy-bitsy biter
67 Units of nautical speed

DOWN

1 Melville captain
2 Limp watch painter
3 Satanic
4 Rind
5 Dickens lad who says "God bless us every one!"
6 Worship
7 ___ Gaga
8 Soap bubbles
9 ___ course (part of boot camp)
10 Throat dangler
11 Wrestling win
12 Outdated
13 With 21-Down, military hawk
21 See 13-Down
22 Key of Beethoven's Symphony No. 7: Abbr.
25 Many flooring installers
26 Show the ropes to
27 Alternatives to purchases
28 Preserves preserver
29 World Cup chant
30 Mascara is applied to them
31 1982 Disney film
32 Devastating hurricane of 2012
33 Pint-size
36 $2,000, if you land on Boardwalk with a hotel

37 Iris's place
39 Spring break activity in Miami Beach or Cabo
42 Beloved, in "Rigoletto"
43 Crazy
46 Web crawler
48 Way overweight
49 Thanksgiving meal
51 Haunted house sound
52 New Age singer from Ireland
53 ___ and bear it
54 Help desk offering
55 Fissure
56 What 1 is to 2 and 2 is to 3
57 Journey to Mecca
58 "Aladdin" prince
59 Chemist's workplace

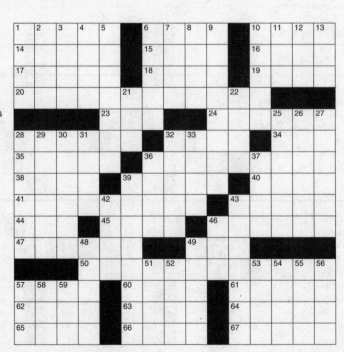

by Dan Margolis

ACROSS

1 Wriggly temptation for a fish
5 To a smaller degree
9 Newswoman Van Susteren
14 Length x width, for a rectangle
15 Rx dosages, e.g.: Abbr.
16 City across the Nile from the Valley of the Kings
17 They might be sealed
18 Apiarist?
20 "Now listen . . ."
22 ___ smasher
23 Trains to Chicago's Loop
24 Flared skirts
26 Org. for some sportswomen
29 Invoice from a souvenir shop?
31 Terse put-down of Sandra's "Gidget" performance?
33 Outrage
34 Toasty
35 King Kong, for one
36 Playlist listing
38 Poorly lit
39 Unsullied
41 ___ Leppard
42 "Paradise Lost" setting
44 Many SAT takers: Abbr.
45 Where to keep divorce papers?
47 Signal Ernie's buddy to step onstage?
51 Blend, as batter
52 Stogies
54 Maiden name preceder
55 Firenze farewell
57 Sitcom segments
59 "Wow, you have violins!"?
62 Influence with higher-ups
63 Long-necked wader
64 Decisive defeat
65 Opera highlight
66 Unlike the proverbial rolling stone

67 ___-serif
68 Microscope part

DOWN

1 Holder for cash and IDs
2 Pro baseball player with an orange-and-black uniform
3 State of rest
4 Lone Ranger accessory
5 Patti in the Grammy Hall of Fame
6 Chef known for "New New Orleans" cuisine
7 17th-century Dutch painter Jan
8 Worrisome org. for a draft dodger
9 Market oversupply
10 Dancer Nureyev
11 Typical specimen

12 Unit of capacity for a bridge
13 17,000-year-old find in France's Lascaux cave
19 Cop's stunner
21 Salon product for a spiky do
25 Dutch cheese
27 Stare open-mouthed
28 Made disappear, in a way
30 Recycling receptacle
32 Title for Maria Theresa of Austria
34 Triumph
36 Quick, suggestive message
37 Badge holders
38 Arnaz of "I Love Lucy"
40 Many a PC cable
41 ___ Plaines, Ill.
43 Look of a room
44 Legal authorities

46 Purple things in several van Gogh paintings
47 Pop-producing toy weapon
48 Continue through time
49 Land, as a fish
50 Electric cars named for an inventor
53 Kind of salami
56 Court fig.
58 Girl's name that's also a 59-Down
59 See 58-Down
60 Maniacal leader?
61 Org. of concern to H&R Block

by Lynn Lempel

ACROSS

1 Doll-making tribe of the Southwest
5 Greatly annoys
10 Long, tedious effort
14 Mathematician Turing
15 Circa
16 Surfer's catch
17 Lively Irish dances
18 Sierra ___ (African land)
19 Supermodel from Somalia
20 "From what ___ seen . . ."
21 Singers Johnny and Fiona?
23 Good dogs for pheasant hunters
25 Billiard stick
26 Craving
27 Feature of the easily offended
32 2015 climate accord city
34 "Thou ___ not . . ."
35 French summer
36 Wildcat with tufted ears
37 Performances by two singers . . . like 21- and 49-Across and 3- and 29-Down?
38 Extinguished, as birthday candles, with "out"
39 Soccer stadium cry
40 Dirt, dust, soot, etc.
41 Soothing ointments
42 Desserts with layered fruit and whipped cream
44 Like fish that are difficult to eat
45 Rap's ___ Wayne
46 Salt's partner in potato chip flavoring
49 Singers Keith and John?
54 GPS option: Abbr.
55 "Va-va-___!"
56 Glittery jewelry
57 Negotiator's goal
58 Alleviate
59 Put out, as a statement
60 Ryan of "Boston Public"
61 Parabola shapes
62 Heads of France
63 Huff

DOWN

1 Ones who've traveled to Mecca
2 Martini garnish
3 Singers Patti and Tina?
4 Opposite of outs
5 In abundance
6 Conspires with
7 Stolen stuff
8 Debussy's "Clair de ___"
9 Aids in sign-lettering
10 Motions left or right on Tinder
11 Home furnishing product with a shade
12 Like the president's office
13 Trait transmitter
21 Govt. rules
22 May or Polly of fiction
24 Colorful cereal
27 "___ fightin' words!"
28 Despise
29 Singers Tori and Al?
30 See 31-Down
31 With 30-Down, brief article in a paper
32 Sit (down) hard
33 Heroine of Jean Auel's "The Clan of the Cave Bear"
34 Attire not usually seen on casual Friday
37 Tool part used to create holes
38 ___ of one's existence
40 Profit
41 James ___ (007)
43 Bad thing to go down in
44 Watches episode after episode of a TV series, say
46 Event location
47 Arcade pioneer
48 Ignited again
49 Colored part of the eye
50 Plane engine's sound when taking off
51 Pear variety
52 Otherwise
53 Main point of an idea
57 Dance club bookings, in brief

by Susan Gelfand

ACROSS

1 Important consideration for investors
5 Attire that may leave the chest bare
11 Barely lit
14 Demands
16 Concluding musical section
17 One of the premier clubs in the Premier League
19 Native New Zealander
20 A wee hour
21 Southern region where blues developed
28 Swift steeds
29 Words said while running out the door, maybe
30 Comics villain ___ Luthor
31 Applesauce
32 Die
34 "Law & Order: SVU" actor
35 Diamonds are weighed in them
37 Item swiped by Indiana Jones at the start of "Raiders of the Lost Ark"
41 Conversed
43 Gerontologist's subject
44 Crank (up)
47 Hill that's steep on one side and gentle on the other
49 Bush - or an anagram of BUSH plus one letter
50 Annual Austin festival
53 Halved
54 Actress Mazar of "Entourage"
55 Arrival and departure locales hinted at by 17-, 21- and 50-Across
63 CBS show with a "New Orleans" spinoff
64 Treasured possession
65 Pitiful
66 Indigenous people of Singapore
67 Mill devices

DOWN

1 Volcano feature
2 ___ moment (shortly)
3 Phishing target: Abbr.
4 Does awesomely
5 Goulashes, e.g.
6 Pilgrimage site in central Italy
7 Wheel groove
8 Unfold, poetically
9 Negative linking word
10 Roamer of the Serengeti
11 "Pray continue . . ."
12 Conceptualize
13 1979 breakout role for Mel Gibson
15 Dominant faith of Iran
16 French filmdom
18 Places where lines meet
21 When repeated, Hawaiian menu item
22 Classic Camaro
23 Sashimi go-with
24 Wow
25 Accept, as a lesser charge
26 Component
27 "How sweet ___!"
33 Cause of tree damage and downed telephone wires
35 Sandwich usually served with toothpicks
36 Answer to the riddle "What force or strength cannot get through / I, with gentle touch, can do"
38 Dreadful, as circumstances
39 Cross to bear
40 Like the group you're in if you're out, for short
42 Sneeze sound
43 Waste container
44 Dwellers east of the Urals
45 One of the friends on "Friends"
46 Foul-smelling
48 Actress Hepburn
51 County divs.
52 Melodic subjects in music
56 Meas. of engine speed
57 ___-la
58 Up to, informally
59 Author LeShan
60 1977 Steely Dan album
61 Stove setting for simmering
62 ___ admin (IT pro)

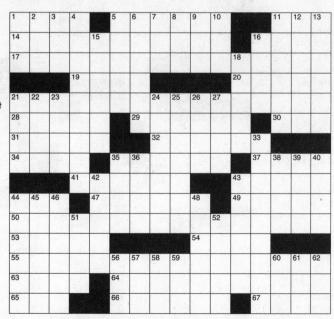

by Jason Flinn

ACROSS

1 Explosions
7 Like the posture of humans
12 Person in a detached state?
13 Hit 2017 Jordan Peele thriller
15 With 25-Down, alchemists' quest in a book released on June 26, 1997
17 Office head
18 Money back
19 Evidence for determining paternity
20 Swear (to)
22 Victory
23 Deadly snakes
26 Units in stables
31 Lion in "The Chronicles of Narnia"
35 Coup d'___
37 Enthusiastic
38 Alphabet chunk after D-E-F
39 Column's counterpart
40 Specialist's vocabulary
41 Distinctive atmosphere
42 Jay once seen nightly
43 Fund, as a chair
44 Coming from two speakers
46 Singer Fitzgerald
48 Bill who's a science expert
50 Small program
55 Lawyers' org.
58 "The Descent of Man" author
61 Widespread
62 Star of the film version of the book referenced in 15-Across/25-Down
65 Comparable to a pin, in a phrase
66 Goes "Ah-choo!"
67 Persistently torment
68 Crafty person at a wheel?

DOWN

1 Given benediction, the old-fashioned way
2 Run out, as a subscription
3 ___ Wednesday
4 Evades
5 Shakespeare's "The Winter's ___"
6 Hoity-toity type
7 Self-centered sort
8 Be in a sorry state?
9 Biblical verb ending
10 Like volleyball that's played jointly by men and women
11 Not go straight
12 "Cat on ___ Tin Roof"
14 Passenger-screening org.
15 Letters on a schedule meaning "We'll let you know"
16 Went on dates with
21 What the Titanic did, famously
24 Father: Fr.
25 See 15-Across
27 Of similar character
28 Advance, as money
29 Toy block brand
30 Cold fall
31 Turkish pooh-bahs
32 Open's opposite
33 Abandoned European capital
34 Not quite closed
36 Soldier who's gone missing
40 Jump
42 Allegiance
45 Cause to be cherished
47 Surgical knife
49 Exemplify humanity, say
51 Contest award
52 Subject of a long sentence?
53 Letters before gees
54 Golf peg
55 Palindromic Nabokov title
56 Big party
57 "___ and the King of Siam"
59 Big stinger
60 Nine-digit fig. on a Social Security card
63 Comparative suffix
64 Tennis umpire's call

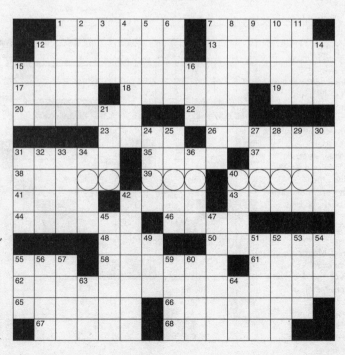

by Brian Greer

ACROSS

1 Exiled leader of 1979
5 Sing smoothly
10 I.R.S. experts
14 Spotted rodent of South America
15 Zoo resident that needs a big tank
16 River of Florence
17 And others, for short
18 Following
19 Word exclaimed with "Get" or "Too"
20 Slight sense that something is seriously shady
23 Minus
24 "Texas tea"
25 Courtroom wear . . . or concern
27 "Just do it" or "I'm lovin' it"
32 One who really brings out the crowds
35 Broody rock genre
36 "Ye" follower on shoppe signs
37 Gene, the singing cowboy
38 Hitters' stats
39 Take advantage of
40 Military unit assembled for sudden attack
42 Generous giving
44 Morales of "Criminal Minds"
45 Jokester
46 Depression-era migrant
48 Fight to the bitter end . . . or a hint to the starts of 20-, 32- and 40-Across
55 "Star Trek: T.N.G." character
56 Stay home for supper
57 "Fine by me"
58 Unwelcome bit of mail
59 Paddle
60 Shakespearean king
61 Artist Warhol
62 Citrusy, e.g.
63 Hamlet, for one

DOWN

1 Eject, as angry words
2 "Thirty days ___ September . . ."
3 Antioxidant-rich berry
4 24,110 years, for plutonium 239
5 Bad state to be in
6 Guitar phrases
7 Chooses
8 Intl. group with two South American members and none in North America
9 "When Harry Met Sally . . ." writer Ephron
10 Exercise on an elliptical machine, informally
11 Middle school math class
12 Annoyingly focused
13 What astronomers call a day on Mars
21 Greek salad topper
22 Florida State athlete, slangily
25 Tortilla chip dip
26 What the River Styx forms the boundary of
27 Bandleader Shaw
28 Quaint dagger
29 Eye woe
30 ___ curiae (friends of the court)
31 Part of the body associated with sneezing, sniffling and snoring
32 Awful-smelling
33 Big mixing containers
34 "___ is not to reason why"
38 Copper alloy used in jewelry
40 State flower of Utah
41 Ireland's Sinn ___
43 Annoying critic
46 In the red
47 Broadway's "___ Boots"
48 Enter
49 Rapper Kanye
50 California's ___ Valley
51 Superhero creator Lee
52 Company that was the first in the U.S. to air a TV ad with a gay couple (1994)
53 Indian flatbread
54 Circular or spiral motion
55 Org. for which Mike Tyson twice held the heavyweight title

by John Guzzetta

ACROSS

1 Tokyo's land
6 How Lindbergh flew across the Atlantic
10 "Atlas Shrugged" author Ayn
14 Spitting bullets
15 Minnesota baseballer
16 Skin soother
17 Air Force smart weapon
20 Atlanta-based cable channel
21 Cry after an errant golf shot
22 Gives a grand speech
23 Like good Scotch
24 Irritated state
25 Pioneering high jump maneuver of the 1960s
29 Not guzzle
32 Sean of "The Lord of the Rings"
33 "Apollo 13" director Howard
34 Superboy's love interest ___ Lang
35 ___ tea (summer drink)
36 Illegal payment
38 Slightly cracked, as a door
39 Superman's love interest Lois ___
40 Fish eggs
41 Jack's fairy tale foe
42 Sign outside a sold-out show
43 Thanksgiving entree
46 Noggin
47 Brewery containers
48 Captain America carries one
51 Wealthy
52 "Elvis ___ left the building"
55 1956 Dean Martin/Jerry Lewis comedy
58 Different
59 With 41-Down, "Alice's Restaurant" singer
60 Ancient region on the Aegean Sea
61 One who might expel a student
62 Say "HEY YOU!," e.g.
63 Writer ___ Allan Poe

DOWN

1 Say "I don't" to instead of "I do"?
2 Yemeni or Omani
3 Hail Mary, for one
4 Enjoyed a buffet
5 "Weapon" with foam darts
6 Solidly built
7 Source of pain, in kidspeak
8 Tupperware top
9 Personal interview
10 Capital of Morocco
11 Oodles
12 U.S. city less than 150 miles from the International Date Line
13 Belles of the ball
18 Ending with church or movie
19 Result of a melting icicle
23 Tolerate
24 Neatnik's opposite
25 Gets an F
26 Award refused by Marlon Brando and George C. Scott
27 Shorthand writer
28 Part of a Happy Meal
29 Pat of "Wheel of Fortune"
30 Asinine
31 Republicans or Democrats
34 Dens
36 Theater district thoroughfare
37 Appropriate word found in 36-Down
41 See 59-Across
43 Depend (on)
44 Luke Perry or Jason Priestley, once
45 ___ Bell (restaurant chain)
46 ___ of Troy
48 Lose, as fur
49 Problem with a sock
50 Rick's love in "Casablanca"
51 Item in a restaurant basket
52 Like a jury that can't reach a decision
53 Himalayas setting
54 One of 50 on the U.S. flag
56 Mine car load
57 Physique, informally

by Randall J. Hartman

ACROSS

1 Covering for leftovers
5 Popular sneakers
9 Pet welfare org.
14 Hairstyle that might have a lot of spray
15 Its first flight went from Geneva to Tel Aviv
16 "Calm down!"
17 Title bootlegger in an F. Scott Fitzgerald novel
19 Fry in a small amount of fat
20 Sick
21 Ones jumping up Down Under, for short
22 Appears to be
23 Gardening tool
24 Édouard who painted "Le Déjeuner sur l'herbe"
25 "I'm here, too"
31 Printing cartridge
32 Tennis star nicknamed "The King of Clay"
33 Russian for "peace"
34 Green-light
35 Tough job for a dry cleaner
36 Skirt that stops at the ankles
37 Country singer Tillis
38 The Hindu "Ramayana" and others
39 Stage, as a play
40 Model with the most Sports Illustrated swimsuit edition covers (5)
43 Amusement park water ride
44 Thumbs-down responses
45 Works hard
46 Ore stratum
48 Big bang letters
51 Cheese from cow's milk
52 "What's the use?"
54 White-plumed marsh dweller
55 ___ Grey tea
56 Song for a coloratura
57 Curving billiards shot
58 Quaker pronoun
59 What the beginnings of 17-, 25-, 40- and 52-Across are each a fourth of, phonetically

DOWN

1 Big name in camera film
2 Fancy stone
3 Pastoral verse
4 Captain's record
5 President, at times
6 In addition
7 Snatches
8 Cunning
9 London football club nicknamed "The Gunners"
10 Anago, at a sushi restaurant
11 Common ingredient in pasta sauce
12 Purrers
13 Firefighter's tool
18 Very loud
22 The Great Tempter
23 Chopper in the Vietnam War
24 Fashionable
25 Backwoods sort
26 Crawling, say
27 Lure
28 Org. that gives out Image Awards and Spingarn Medals
29 President who launched the war on drugs
30 Land celebrated on March 17
31 São ___ and Príncipe
35 Sends unwanted email
36 Dishevel
38 Attempt to copy
39 ___ code (discount provider)
41 Drops a few G's, say?
42 Allow
45 "Julius Caesar" costume
46 Persian leader
47 Jane who falls for Edward Rochester
48 Directional word, for short
49 Justice Gorsuch
50 Highchair surface
51 Real beauty
52 Rainy
53 ___ Mahal

by Mangesh Ghogre and Brendan Emmett Quigley

ACROSS

1 Emancipation Proclamation prez
4 One of the senses
9 Sound from a would-be test cheater
13 Apple computers
15 Ancient land in Asia Minor
16 The Bruins of the N.C.A.A.
17 Colorful top often worn with a lei
19 ___ and cons
20 "Attack, Bowser!"
21 Part of a grove
23 Night of anticipation
24 Tel Aviv skyscraper that was the first to be built in the Mideast
28 ___-splitting (really loud)
29 ___ de Janeiro
30 Holy sanctuary
31 "Absolutely, amigo!"
33 Yep's opposite
36 Played a part
37 Long, tranquil period ushered in by the emperor Augustus
40 "That's a shame"
43 Roasting rod
44 Fire, as from a job
48 Kit that may include colored pencils and a stencil
50 ___-tac-toe
52 "That's all ___ wrote"
53 Orbiter from 1986 to 2001
57 Links org.
58 Grow weary
59 Sticky secretion
60 Paying close attention
62 Ancient dream of humanity that's hinted at by the starts of 17-, 24-, 37- and 53-Across (in Hawaiian, Hebrew, Latin and Russian, respectively)

65 "Lucky Jim" author Kingsley
66 California's Santa ___ Derby
67 Went kaput
68 Where dirty dishes pile up
69 Impoverished
70 Help with the dishwashing, say

DOWN

1 Accumulates
2 "South Pacific" show tune
3 Fuel-efficient vehicles
4 "___ the season . . ."
5 "___-la-la!"
6 Bring together
7 High, wispy clouds
8 Critics who can't be pleased
9 Kitten : cat :: ___ : dog
10 "Oh darn, I give up!"
11 Ljubljana resident
12 Used a stun gun on
14 Poet/illustrator Silverstein
18 God of love
22 Joel Coen's filmmaking brother
25 Coquette
26 British wastelands
27 Killer whales
32 Bridge declaration when not bidding
34 Partner of Snap and Crackle
35 Gives off, as light
38 Skilled
39 Going ___ (fighting)
40 Pete with seven Wimbledon championships

41 Paper-folding craft
42 Put on one's seat belt
45 "Let me reiterate . . ."
46 Finer in quality
47 Defeater of Nixon in 1960
49 Disputed island in the China Sea
51 Incessantly complain
54 Witch
55 Shiver-inducing
56 Ticked (off)
61 "For shame!"
63 Inc., in England
64 Period on Venus that's longer than a year on Venus (!)

by Timothy Polin

ACROSS

1. Make the grade
5. Matchmaking site since 1997
10. Working hard
14. Introductory painting class
15. Assign, as blame
16. Done, in Dijon
17. Hunky-dory
20. ___ Arbor, Mich.
21. Turkish for "lord"
22. Borrower's letters
23. Perennially strong entrant at the Winter Olympics: Abbr.
24. America, for example, which has a "Cup" named after it
26. Untouchable one
29. Tennis star Arthur
30. Off-road wheels, briefly
31. Screenwriter Ephron
32. Ladies' man
34. Stockpiles
36. Victoria and David Beckham, e.g. . . . or what 17-, 26-, 47- and 57-Across each have, in a way
38. Dangers
40. Sleep clinic concern
41. SpaceX founder Musk
42. Found really neat
43. The Rolling Stones or Smashing Pumpkins
47. Stayed calm
51. Big name in nail polish
52. Something that's definite?
53. Numbskull
54. Canon camera
56. Workout target, for short
57. Pre-employment screening
61. Vision: Prefix
62. Come in second
63. Cold drink at Burger King
64. Former C.I.A. director Porter ___
65. Kills time
66. War vet's affliction, for short

DOWN

1. Fruit in som tam salad
2. Sports centers
3. Stem the flow of
4. [not my mistake]
5. Picture file format
6. "Twister" or "San Andreas" film genre
7. Santa ___ winds
8. Gin's partner
9. Home of the Ewoks
10. Togo's home: Abbr.
11. No-win situation
12. Briefly
13. "I remember when . . ."
18. Bowler, e.g.
19. Stage signal
25. Katniss Everdeen, in "The Hunger Games"
27. California roll ingredient
28. Swab analysis sites
30. Iowa college town
33. A fly-by-night?
34. Like some juries
35. Unlock, to a poet
36. Guards
37. Luxury
38. Natural fuel source
39. Nickname of the Mexican drug lord Joaquín Guzmán
44. Facet
45. "Uncle!" criers, maybe
46. Punched out
48. Follow relentlessly
49. Wrist bones
50. Long past
51. YouTube full-screen mode exit key
55. Laudatory poetry
58. Boxing victories, briefly
59. Delta competitor: Abbr.
60. Trendy

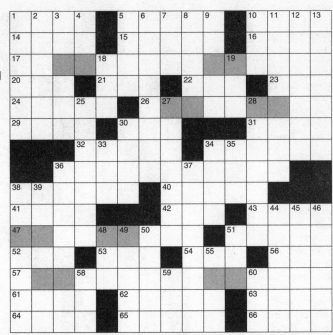

by Zhouqin Burnikel

ACROSS

1 Building material for the first little pig
6 Some bank offerings, for short
9 ___ and cheese
12 Swim meet coverage?
13 Nancy who solves mysteries
14 Words said at the altar
15 President's plane
17 ___-Mex
18 Roadside stops
19 Wrestling for 400-pounders
20 Rod-shaped bacterium
22 Broadway's "___ Miz"
23 Cry before "You're out!"
25 Dorm figs.
26 Actor Hemsworth of "The Hunger Games"
27 Material for a tight-fitting glove
30 "Up top!"
35 Landed, as on a branch
36 Actions on the dance floor
37 "Mmm-hmm, mmm-hmm"
38 Conclusion of a close World Series
40 Photographer Adams
41 Flair
42 Brand of sheepskin boots
43 Ecstatic
48 He-sheep
51 Beauty's partner, with "the"
52 Charged particles
53 Martial art that's an Olympic sport
54 Big feature on a donkey
55 Miscellany . . . or a description of the final words in 15-, 23-, 30-, 38- and 43-Across
58 Since Jan. 1

59 Word repeated in "It's ___, all ___!"
60 Tax cheats' fears
61 "Hel-l-lp!"
62 Suffix with differ
63 Insurance company with a lizard mascot

DOWN

1 Backbone
2 Shore birds
3 Officials crying "Offside" and "Pass interference"
4 Commotion
5 Opposite of bests
6 No-good thief
7 Lair
8 Hon
9 Sometimes good, sometimes bad
10 "Hello" singer of 2015
11 Gumption
12 Take a yacht out
13 Singer Lovato
16 Scoundrel
21 Rubbing the wrong way?
23 "Wailing" instrument
24 Stately shade trees
25 Gives a new account of
27 Annoying feature of an online stream
28 In the manner of
29 Means of tracking workers' hours
30 www.healthcare.___
31 "Now ___ seen it all!"
32 Restroom sign
33 Flying geese formation
34 Sea slitherer
36 It's fixed for a prix fixe meal
39 Principe's sister island
40 6 or so, for first graders

42 Release from being caught on a nail, say
43 Adheres to, as a rule
44 Old-fashioned "Awesome!"
45 "I ___ see that coming!"
46 What smells
47 Pigs ___ blanket
48 Like some ancient characters
49 Embellish
50 What rolling stones don't gather
53 Force-ful characters?
56 Cacophony
57 Like some library books and babies

by Tom McCoy

ACROSS

1 Braided Jewish bread
8 Some punches
13 Fill to the gills
14 Stay faithful
15 Takes stock?
16 Colonial-era headgear
17 Cleverness thought of too late to use
19 "___ a Mad, Mad, Mad, Mad World" (1963 film)
20 Country singer Keith
21 Former inits. for Spike TV
22 Prefix with tourism
23 Department store founder R. H. ___
24 Cost of admission
25 The "A" of I.P.A.
26 Place to find a pen and teller
27 Wretched
30 Flexible contract provision
33 Gets back together, as a class
34 Wasteful government spending
35 Seating with hymnals
36 "As an aside . . . ," in a text
37 ___ Martin (Cognac maker)
38 It can go for a buck
39 "Golly!"
40 Cartoon character who explores with Boots
41 "Golly!"
42 Straight-shooting
45 Dessert brand
46 Dressing up as a fictional character with others
50 Bathroom units
51 Malevolent look
52 Shelters
53 Leaves the union

DOWN

1 TV show that spawned an exhibit at Chicago's Museum of Science and Industry
2 ___ Solo
3 Off-road ride, for short
4 Gives a false story
5 Endures
6 Lead-in to boy or girl
7 Wondering "Should I? Should I not?"
8 Floral necklaces
9 Latin phrase used listlessly?
10 Discouraged
11 City NW of Genoa
12 Posted
14 Hee-haw
16 Dessert chain
18 The Who's "Tommy," e.g.
19 Freeze frame?
22 Otherwise
23 Peter who wrote "Serpico"
24 Ordinary people
25 ___ Lingus
26 Played, as a trumpet
27 Foretell the future by using a crystal ball
28 Stereotypical response from a shrink
29 Overnight delivery?
31 Entrance room where guests wait
32 Good date movies
37 Need for tug-of-war
38 Rounded patch of color on an animal coat
39 Small annoyances
40 Cost of membership
41 "That's ___ to my ears"
42 Mount of Greek myth
43 Jazz great Fitzgerald
44 Peace symbol
47 Had the helm
48 Affirmative vote
49 Affirmative

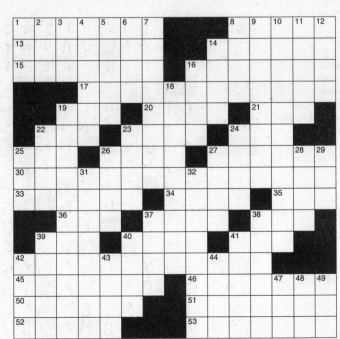

by Michael Hawkins

ACROSS

1 Green condiment served with sushi
7 Hyphen's longer cousin
13 Boxer George who lost the Rumble in the Jungle
14 Excessively praised
16 Brand of pasta
17 What golfers with equal numbers of squares and circles on their scorecards shoot
18 "So that's your trick!"
19 Took the wrong way?
21 "Exodus" hero
22 Parceled (out)
25 "TiK ___" (Ke$ha hit)
26 Effect's counterpart
28 Ramen product
31 Stream
32 Overnight lodges
33 Split-___ soup
36 Ouzo flavoring
38 "Thar ___ blows!"
41 Churchgoers, collectively
43 Mo. when daylight saving time ends
44 Milo of "The Verdict"
46 Taj Mahal city
47 Helped
49 Fisheye or zoom
50 Buyer's bottom line
52 Former full-size Buick
54 Mistakes
55 N'awlins sandwiches
56 "Sesame Street" Muppet with wings and a magic wand
60 Donated
62 Less common
63 Punk rock's ___ Pop
66 Figure skating jump
67 Small bit of land in the ocean
68 Back of the neck
69 Shout
70 Molecule components
71 Annoying insect

DOWN

1 Celebratory shout
2 ___ Palmer (drink made with lemonade and iced tea)
3 "Oh, yeah? ___ who?"
4 I love, in Latin
5 Prohibits
6 Competing with the goal of victory
7 Daredevil in the Motorcycle Hall of Fame
8 Church area
9 "With all ___ respect . . ."
10 Clothing retailer ___ Taylor
11 Capital of Minnesota
12 Opposite of a life coach?
13 Hobbit played by Elijah Wood
15 Helps with the dishes
20 Sound that a punch in the gut elicits
23 North Pole worker
24 Postpone
26 Alternative to a co-op
27 Commercials
29 Male delivery
30 Pi's first digit after the decimal
33 Carpentry tool
34 Rarin' to go
35 Business for Delta or Southwest
37 Lawn section
38 Wisconsin city on Lake Michigan
39 Fonda or Ford
40 Facilitates
42 Fast-food chain with the slogan "Live más"
45 Applying thickly, with "on"
47 Ancient kingdom whose capital was Nineveh
48 Leaves
51 Sphere
53 Have a bawl
57 Playbill listing
58 Folk singer Guthrie
59 Regard
60 The "G" of L.G.B.T.
61 Firefighter's tool
64 High no. for a valedictorian
65 Nevertheless

by Peter Gordon

ACROSS

1 Discharge, as from a volcano
5 Isn't rigid in one's ways
11 Chrysler truck
14 Height: Prefix
15 Protective embankment
16 He said that ambient music "must be as ignorable as it is interesting"
17 Was loved by
20 Zoë of "Avatar"
21 Didn't buy, say
22 Know-it-all
25 Jason's vessel, in myth
28 Underside of an 8-Down
29 Giga- × 1,000
32 No holds ___
35 Captain Nemo's vessel
38 Oral health org.
39 Comment after a fortuitous happening
41 Sound of reproach
42 It isn't recorded in a walk-off win
44 First female speaker of the House
46 Chuck of "Meet the Press"
47 Louisa May Alcott's "___ Boys"
49 Erelong
50 Frequently going from one post to another
55 Christmas ornament, e.g.
57 Puts in a box
61 Evangelize . . . or what this puzzle's circled squares do?
64 Equal at the start?
65 Enthusiastic response to "Who wants dessert?"
66 Family history, e.g.
67 Gen ___
68 Like emotions just after a tragedy
69 Craft company with a 2015 I.P.O.

DOWN

1 ___ Club
2 Defendant's entry
3 Shortening for a bibliographer
4 House of Elizabeth II
5 The Hartford competitor
6 Note in the E major scale
7 Fly through, as a test
8 Hound's "hand"
9 Nuisance in an online comments section
10 Shopping trip one may later regret
11 Variety show host of 1951–71
12 Cost to get in
13 Emotional state
18 Highlander's headwear
19 Milk: Prefix
23 What gives you the right to bare arms?
24 "There will come ___ . . ."
25 Toward the rear
26 NPR segment?
27 One voting to indict or not
30 Model-turned-actress Rene
31 Welcome at the front door
33 Certain office desk setup
34 Hip-hop's Kris Kross or OutKast
36 Call balls and strikes, informally
37 End of August?
40 Title canine in a Stephen King book
43 Baked brick
45 Chef Emeril
48 Is a leadfoot
51 ___ House (Washington landmark)
52 Ibsen's "___ Gabler"
53 Gold standard?
54 Pvt.'s superior
55 Vitamin whose name rhymes with a car engine
56 Chapel recess
58 Dustup
59 Dr.'s orders
60 Knock dead at the comedy club
62 Haul on a U-Haul
63 Rush

by Alex Vratsanos

48

Note: When this puzzle is finished, read the circled letters roughly clockwise, starting with the first letter of 68-Across, to spell the name of an appropriate landmark.

ACROSS

1 "Star ___ Beyond" (2016 film)
5 "Are you interested in doin' this?"
10 Livens (up)
14 Harvard's archrival
15 Taking a nap, say
16 "Night" author Wiesel
17 Downtown 68-Across attraction
20 Without guaranteed payment
21 Big brand of glue
22 Vientiane's country
24 ___ B'rith
25 Spiked medieval clubs
28 Mai ___ (cocktail)
30 March 17 honoree, for short
34 Starting from
35 Bamboo-eating bear
37 Stubborn animal
38 Gold, frankincense or myrrh, for baby Jesus
39 Soda bottle measure
40 Grade A items in the dairy aisle
41 Clumsy person
42 68-Across baseball player
44 Devour
45 2,000 pounds
47 French edict city
49 Mathematician whose name sounds like a fuel ship
51 Fills to capacity
52 Trash or compost
54 Suffix with real or surreal
56 Tree's support system
59 "What'd you say?"
60 Pancake-flipping implement
63 Large tea container
64 Answer at the altar
65 Ship featured in a 1997 megafilm
66 Actress Vardalos
67 Move really fast
68 City that's the subject of this puzzle
69 Pomeranian, e.g.

DOWN

1 Spell-checker target
2 Common 68-Across forecast
3 Antlered animals
4 Liberal's favorite road sign?
5 Radioer's word after "Roger"
6 Santa ___ winds
7 "The Voice" airer
8 Hillary Clinton ___ Rodham
9 Some slogan writers
10 Chivalrous offer
11 Sommer of 1960s–'70s films
12 Waterfront 68-Across location
13 Dips below the horizon
18 Small, spherical vegetables
19 "Woe is me!"
23 It goes from one story to another
24 Obama's veep
25 Mr. ___ (nearsighted toon)
26 From east of the Urals
27 Business on every block in 68-Across, so it's said
29 Opposed to
31 Body of water that 68-Across is on
32 Fish tank buildup
33 Exams
35 Vehicle with wings and a nose
36 Gladiator fight site
42 Pesters repeatedly
43 Hurry of modern life
46 King who died in his late teens
48 "The Matrix" hero
50 Cowboy's rope
51 Fire-eating, for one
52 Expert, informally
53 Automaker with a four-ring logo
55 On-base percentage, e.g.
57 Half of a sextet
58 Stocking problem
61 Dessert divided into slices
62 ___ Wayne, rapper with the #1 hit "Lollipop"

by David Steinberg

ACROSS

1 Zin alternative
4 With 6-Down, "Dancing Queen" musical
9 One of the Three Musketeers
14 Baton Rouge sch.
15 "See you!"
16 Main impact
17 "Shocking!," to an astronomer?
19 Camping craft
20 Secures, as an area, with "off"
21 Duracell designation
23 Cincinnati sitcom station
24 Mine finds
25 "Shocking!," to an Ohio tourist?
28 Gen ___
29 Zest
30 Pommes frites seasoning
31 Stimpy's TV pal
32 Strange
34 "Nothing runs like a ___" (ad slogan)
36 "Shocking!," to a seamstress?
39 Childish comeback
41 Primitive fishing tool
42 Teachers' org.
43 Sloth, for one
46 What some shoulders and pants do
47 English head
50 "Shocking!," to a teetotaler?
53 Something to watch on the telly, with "the"
54 End in ___
55 White wine aperitif
56 Make a case (for)
57 Wanders
59 "Shocking!," to a Thanksgiving guest?
62 Jurassic Park inhabitants, for short
63 Mandel of "America's Got Talent"
64 Uno + due
65 One may be rolling or skipped
66 Bit of campaign nastiness
67 Multivolume ref.

DOWN

1 Bleach brand
2 Enjoying Fleet Week, say
3 Part of a pinball machine
4 Atomic ___
5 Big letters in home security
6 See 4-Across
7 "Slow and steady wins the race," e.g.
8 Some lab tests
9 "The Goldbergs" network
10 Net that netted Dory in "Finding Nemo"
11 Hid out, with "down"
12 Yet to be delivered
13 Start of a manual
18 "By all means"
22 Got rid of the munchies
25 Marijuana, slangily
26 Onetime Ron Howard role
27 Racetrack has-been
29 Boehner's predecessor as House leader
32 "Strange Magic" band, for short
33 Mag heads
35 At any time, to poets
36 Lingua di Luigi
37 Quiet place to pray
38 Tail end
39 To the center
40 Make sure something gets done
44 It's usually not erasable
45 Sounds from a stable
47 Smooth, in music
48 Entirety of a composer's works
49 Followed instructions
51 Car that's hardly a peach
52 Racetrack sound
53 "I can't f-f-feel my f-f-feet!"
56 Ending with teen
58 Chicago-to-Indianapolis dir.
60 Be in the red
61 24 horas

by Jay Kaskel

ACROSS

1 Inn, informally
6 "No ___" (menu phrase)
9 Sight on the coast of Norway
14 Ancient Greek marketplace
15 It's roughly 78% nitrogen
16 Slow, in music
17 Put a new price on
18 Fury
19 Animal that frolics in streams
20 Feature of the big city
23 XXX-XX-XXXX fig.
24 Fawn's mother
25 Japanese port city
28 Practical joke show first aired in 1948
32 "I goofed!"
35 Egg cell
36 Coq au ___
37 Advocate for the 50-and-over crowd
38 What card dealers deal
40 Competed
41 Reggae relative
42 "Beloved" author Morrison
43 Violet variety
44 Secret military operation
48 Arena, e.g.
49 Inquire
50 A, in Acapulco
53 Speaker of the last words of 20-, 28- and 44-Across
57 A lot of them can be found on a lot
60 Be under the weather
61 Sacred choral work
62 The first one begins "Blessed is the one who does not walk in step with the wicked"
63 Madhouse
64 Double-clicks on, say
65 Looks after
66 "To ___ is human . . ."
67 Like almost every major character on "The Big Bang Theory"

DOWN

1 Cutting remarks
2 Golden ___ (elderly sorts)
3 Away from the office
4 Long inhaling of a cigarette
5 Capital of Iraq
6 Took to the post office
7 iPhone assistant
8 The kid in "Diary of a Wimpy Kid"
9 Detritus at sea
10 Detritus at sea
11 Toronto's prov.
12 GPS offering: Abbr.
13 Palme ___ (top prize at Cannes)
21 Weight unit for a bridge
22 ___-pocus
26 Actor Costner or Spacey
27 Leo : lion :: ___ : ram
28 Bit of attire sometimes worn backward
29 Greek column style
30 Object made obsolescent by streaming
31 Tennis's Murray
32 Not fem.
33 Comedian Smirnoff
34 Courageous
38 Ritz-Carlton, for one
39 Good "Wheel of Fortune" purchase for the answer PANAMA CANAL
40 Vehicle for a painter or plumber
42 "You get what you pay for" and others
43 Character on a collectible card
45 Wrap around
46 Le Carré's "Tinker ___ Soldier Spy"
47 Tel Aviv's land: Abbr.
50 Speak
51 On and on
52 Pretentious
54 Labyrinth
55 Designer Christian
56 Manage
57 Appropriate
58 Employ
59 Something that might be picked up at the beach

by Kevin Christian

ACROSS

1 Row
5 Worn out
10 The Kleenex of cotton swabs
14 Predator of dolphins
15 Press secretary ___ Huckabee Sanders
16 ___ Major (Big Dipper's constellation)
17 4/4
19 Smidgen
20 Prepare to be knighted
21 Indianapolis-to-Cleveland dir.
22 To whom "break a leg" is said
23 Period in Congress
25 Basketball highlight
27 11/11
32 Hay and such for farm animals
36 "The Raven" poet
37 Prefix with space
38 Girlfriends in Paris
39 "Great Expectations" protagonist
40 Tiptoe, perhaps
41 Drug informant, informally
42 "The Lord of the Rings" baddie
43 Walk like a two-year-old, say
44 20/20
47 Trolley
48 Division of baseball's N.L. or A.L.
53 Always trying to get one's way
56 Green: Prefix
58 Wear away
59 European automaker
60 50/50
62 "The Simpsons" character with a palindromic name
63 "Sexy" woman in a Beatles song
64 Start running

65 Butcher's cut
66 Put in office
67 You are, south of the border

DOWN

1 Argyle pair
2 Lying on one's stomach
3 Zeniths
4 Takes the wildness out of
5 I.R.S. digits: Abbr.
6 It lasts 20 years
7 The Emerald Isle
8 Say "When I was with my good friend Barack last week . . . ," e.g.
9 Word ignored when alphabetizing
10 Something that gives you a sinking feeling
11 Home-run run
12 Analogy words
13 Jack of the old "Tonight Show"
18 Mount of ___ (Jerusalem landmark)
22 Advice-giving Landers
24 "___ the land of the free . . ."
26 Dubai's home: Abbr.
28 Some long novels
29 Monopoly card
30 Asia's disappearing ___ Sea
31 Oxen connector
32 Dracula's biter
33 Vizquel with 11 Gold Gloves
34 Like some straits
35 Olympic event won by Bruce Jenner in 1976 and Ashton Eaton in 2012 and 2016
39 Really, really old
40 One of 154 by Shakespeare
42 Eggs
43 Lowest digit
45 Word repeated before "again"
46 Like Warhol's Marilyn Monroe painting
49 Onetime HBO series set in New Orleans
50 Standard dog name
51 "Skyfall" singer
52 Periods after Mardi Gras
53 Summer hangout
54 "I've had it ___ here!"
55 Org. in Carl Sagan's "Contact"
57 Surrender
60 Suffix in many language names
61 Ready

by Dan Flanagan

ACROSS

1 Where holsters go
5 Torso muscles, briefly
9 Turn into a pretzel
14 ___ palm (tree with a healthful berry)
15 Automobile rod
16 Italian scooter brand
17 Thrifty or Budget offering
19 Keep occupied, as a phone line
20 Meal option #1
22 007, for one
23 "___ of a gun!"
24 Cheer made with a pompom
25 Moo goo gai pan pan
26 Brit's teapot cover
28 Consume
31 Meal option #2
35 Broadcasts
36 Hawaiian garland
37 Overdue
38 Meal option #3
43 Pig's home
44 Where hay is stored in a barn
45 Path that wheels keep following
46 French for "him"
47 Completely finishing this crossword, to you
48 Residue of burning
51 Weekly occurrence when 20-, 31- and 38-Across might be consumed
56 Dance to some Johann Strauss music
57 Path for cyclists
58 Fit to be tied
59 La ___ Tar Pits
60 Blueprint
61 Things producing red hair or blue eyes
62 Stitched
63 Sicilian volcano

DOWN

1 In ___ way
2 Freeze over, as airplane wings
3 Colorful flower also known as heartsease
4 ___ Lord (Jedi's foe)
5 Big oaf
6 One no longer in the pen
7 Raw bar offering
8 Belgrade native
9 Some light foldable tables
10 Put on the scale
11 "Understood"
12 Cowboy boot attachment
13 Faucet
18 Illegal burning
21 ___ Major (Great Bear)
25 The Dairy State: Abbr.
26 Peek at someone else's paper, e.g.
27 Actress Lena of "Chocolat"
28 Alike, in Paris
29 ___-Defamation League
30 ___ kwon do (martial art)
31 Sediment
32 Say grace, e.g.
33 First symbol on a musical staff
34 Landed
35 Torso muscles, briefly
39 They're all thumbs
40 Directive in a pasta recipe
41 Like the peninsula seized by Russia in 2014
42 "Mankind's greatest blessing," per Mark Twain
46 Espresso drink
47 Like an off-center tie
48 XXX
49 The Devil
50 "Laughing" animal
51 Mother horse
52 Flair
53 Recedes, as the tide
54 Father horse
55 "Negatory"
56 Dome topper?

by Rich Proulx

53

ACROSS

1 Line of clothing
7 Random guess
11 Deg. that requires a defense
14 Japanese floor mat
15 "Didn't see ya there!"
16 Garden row maker
17 Old video game consoles
18 Stamp collector?
20 "Total Recall" director Wiseman
21 Enthusiastic Spanish assent
23 Like sports crowds during a close game
24 Because of
27 "Hail Mary, full of grace . . . ," e.g.
28 Record collector?
32 Significant
33 Showy purple bloom
34 Energy measurement, for short
37 Cranberry picking sites
38 Who famously said "I'm not a crook"
40 Media slant
41 Prefix with -metric
42 Calliope or Euterpe
43 Play a fife
45 Bill collector?
47 Tiered Eastern temple
50 Something measured by holding fingers on the wrist
51 Trojan War epic
52 Galileo's hometown
54 A detour offers a different one: Abbr.
57 Shell collector?
59 Undoing of legislation
62 Mobile CPR provider
63 Hit the ___ (go to bed)
64 Intimidates
65 Morse code plea

66 Multiple jobs, metaphorically
67 It might come with a cherry on top

DOWN

1 Slanted in print: Abbr.
2 Five ThirtyEight creator Silver
3 Rousing audience response, informally
4 Something popped on a plane
5 Parisian pal
6 Pageant title since 1983
7 Soaks (up)
8 Cuisine with tom kha gai soup
9 Sighed sounds
10 Places serving salades et sandwiches
11 Hypocrite, say

12 Derby entrant
13 Hold off
19 Word after mountain or before season
22 Platform for Siri
25 Some chain pizzerias
26 Sinus doc
27 Players bringing the ball up the court
28 Desert along the Silk Road
29 Subjects of some fuzzy photos, for short
30 Philly pro
31 ___ hug
34 Final and unhappy outcome
35 Fish story
36 ___ interface
39 Kinda sorta
40 Big enchilada
42 Frenzied race

44 Coconut product
45 Wool, for a sheep
46 Short albums, for short
47 Puff pieces?
48 San Antonio mission
49 Main points
52 Treaty
53 Ticks off
55 "Toodles!"
56 "What ___ is new?"
58 Cry of shear terror?
60 It's in la Seine
61 The clue for 58-Down, e.g. [sorry!]

by Zhouqin Burnikel

ACROSS

1 Won every game
6 Fast-food chain with a red-haired girl in its logo
12 Unhappy
15 2008 Pixar film about a robot
16 Dolts
17 Comedian Philips
18 Feet in the city? (3 wds.)
20 PC part, for short
21 Signify
22 Baldwin famous for his Donald Trump impersonation
23 Something screwed into a lamp
24 Friendly Communist ghost? (3 wds.)
29 Singer Midler
31 "Sure thing!"
32 Angels' headwear
33 Close tightly
36 Adore, cutesily
38 "Can you give an example . . . ?"
39 Something to ____ mind . . . in 18-, 24-, 47- and 58-Across
40 ____ one's time
41 Tree whose name sounds like a letter of the alphabet
42 City in southern France
43 Principal principle
44 ____ monkey
46 Mopes
47 Slim monarch who gets around fast? (3 wds.)
51 "Do ____ others . . ."
52 Containers for cookies or sewing supplies
53 Equipment for a motorcycle jump
57 Word after Holiday or Comfort
58 Head off to stare at some pictures? (3 wds.)
62 General who's 34-Down spelled backward

63 With nothing omitted
64 Scents
65 Sample
66 Patronize, as a hotel
67 Engender

DOWN

1 Done the backstroke, e.g.
2 Ending with silver or soft
3 "Able was I ere I saw ____"
4 Food for whales
5 Hamilton's bill
6 Brandish, as a weapon
7 Lawn tool
8 Sister's daughter
9 ____ Juan (lover)
10 Financial spreadsheet column: Abbr.
11 Air-escaping-from-a-tire sound
12 It's safe to click on a computer

13 Wave measurements
14 "But what if I'm wrong?" feeling
19 Narrow street
23 It guards a dribbler
25 "____ a long story"
26 2016 Nobel laureate Bob
27 Vichyssoise or borscht
28 Young pooch
29 Player on first, second or third
30 Inventor of the cotton gin
32 Bales in a loft
33 "Oh, be quiet!"
34 Fish that's 62-Across spelled backward
35 "A long time ____ in a galaxy far, far away . . ."
37 Dog doc
39 Praise highly
40 Serbia's capital
42 Disapproving syllable
43 Wine cask
45 ____-friendly

46 Mexican's emphatic assent
47 Bedcover made of patches
48 Computer-savvy office fellow
49 Wafer brand
50 Prepared to pop the question, perhaps
54 Wide-eyed
55 ____ mortal
56 "Hey you!"
58 Audience members for a U.S.O. show
59 Toronto's province: Abbr.
60 "Son ____ gun!"
61 Group carrying torches and pitchforks

by Tom McCoy

ACROSS

1 Containers at chocolate factories
5 Southern city just south of a national forest with the same name
10 Shout after a stressful week
14 Mrs. Peacock's game
15 Cello bow application
16 Plead with, say
17 Fire hydrant attachment
18 Managed to irk
19 It's a big blow
20 Pixar's "Monsters, ___"
21 Orally
23 Nonverbal "yes"
24 R&B singer Bryson
26 ___ Levin, author of "Rosemary's Baby"
27 Windows precursor
29 Undergraduate law deg.
30 Nothing
31 Clumsy fellow
32 Egg ___ yung (Chinese dish)
33 Newborn horses
35 "This instant!"
37 Make an approach like a bird of prey
39 Common churchyard conifer
42 Destiny
43 Spiritual center, in yoga
44 Look for
45 ___-Man
48 "Nothing for me, thanks"
49 Adm. Horatio Nelson, for one
52 Superexcited
55 Glowing bit in a fire
56 Aborted plan
60 Rorschach test shape
61 Show leniency toward
62 "The very ___!"

63 No-brainer?
64 Freak out
65 Champagne bottle stopper
66 "Truer words have never been spoken!"
67 Thus far
68 It "marches on its stomach," per Napoleon

DOWN

1 TV blocking device
2 Companionless
3 Where the Crimson Tide play
4 Lay eyes on
5 Out-of-control revelry
6 Get a close-up of by camera
7 City almost at the end of the Columbia River

8 In a ceremonial manner
9 Hard-to-undo tie
10 Yank
11 Red River Valley city in the upper Midwest
12 House that's cool to live in?
13 Puts money in, as a meter
21 Go up and down, as a buoy
22 Plan for hosp. patients
25 State university city in the Midwest
28 Sunny city with a famous pier
32 "Here are my thoughts," online
33 Something thrown in frustration
34 1/60 of a min.
36 Used to be

37 Calypso-influenced genre
38 "I'd rather go naked than wear fur" org.
40 Fan sound
41 Consume
45 Argentine grassland
46 Original eastern terminus of the Erie Canal
47 French sweetie
50 Italian motor scooter
51 Not hunched over
52 Group with the hit "Waterloo"
53 Grab (onto)
54 Exude, as charm
57 Musk, e.g.
58 Infection cause
59 Tasting of wood, as some chardonnays

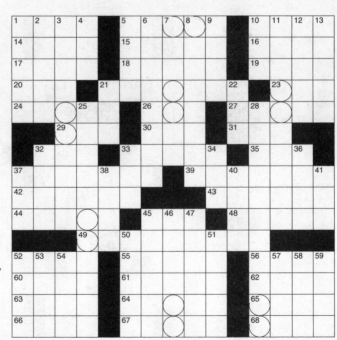

by Timothy Polin

56

ACROSS

1 Battery fluid
5 Wide keyboard key
10 Loch ___ monster
14 Variety of wrestling
15 Overcharge
16 Loads and loads
17 Extremely obstinate
20 Kathmandu's land
21 Little League coach, often
22 Ushered
23 Rikki-tikki-___ (Kipling mongoose)
25 City in Spain or Ohio
26 Person who's talented but not versatile
31 "To be, or not to be" speaker
32 Sleep like ___
33 To the ___ (fully)
36 Charades player, essentially
37 Fortuneteller's card
39 Road shoulder
40 Foxy
41 Negligible
42 Rest of the afternoon
44 Notable (and grammatically incorrect) declaration by Mr. Bumble in "Oliver Twist"
46 Top dogs
49 Curb, with "in"
50 Urban's opposite
51 Staple of sci-fi filmmaking, for short
53 Web site?
57 Acting haughtily and pompously
60 Fell to the seabed
61 Figure made by a figure skater
62 Document with the line "I hereby bequeath . . ."
63 Work units, in physics
64 Chooses actors for
65 London's ___ Coward Theater

DOWN

1 The first "A" of N.A.A.C.P.: Abbr.
2 Like puppies and kittens
3 "No need to wake me"
4 Fight (with)
5 "I" problem?
6 Light-skinned and blond, say
7 Fish that's a sushi staple
8 "Holy mackerel!"
9 Hi-___ monitor
10 To wit
11 Escape capture by
12 Not liquid or gaseous
13 ___ pad (reporter's notebook)
18 Trumpet
19 "Moving right ___ . . ."
24 Food, informally
25 1982 comedy for which Jessica Lange won Best Supporting Actress
26 Units of resistance
27 Execute perfectly, as a routine
28 TV award
29 Destiny
30 West Bank inits.
33 Big butte
34 ___ and crafts
35 Big workday for Saint Nick
38 Not feel 100%
39 Boston, informally
41 Oil-producing rock
43 ___ Thomas, N.B.A. Hall-of-Famer
44 "Appreciate it!"
45 Orville or Wilbur
46 Came up
47 Like some eclipses
48 Point on antlers
51 "Pet" that's a plant
52 Play dates?
54 The Supremes, e.g.
55 ___ of Man
56 Prison compartment
58 Instant, for short
59 Elevations: Abbr.

by Dan Margolis

ACROSS

1 Staple of Chinese cuisine
5 Submit tax forms the modern way
10 Jockey's accessory
14 Actor Epps
15 Charles or Ray after whom a chair is named
16 Onetime Ritz rival
17 Classic game needing no equipment
20 Event name suffix
21 One of the friends on "Friends"
22 Doing a pirouette, say
23 Start of the Lord's Prayer
24 Common baby ailment
26 You might not want to touch something with this
33 Diarist Nin
34 Edward James ___, star of "Stand and Deliver"
35 Word before coat or rat
36 Contents of Pandora's box
37 High winds?
38 El ___ (weather phenomenon)
39 "N.Y. State of Mind" rapper
40 Briefly, after "in"
41 Brand of candy hearts
42 1965 Beatles hit
45 Equine, in totspeak
46 Letters on exploding boxes in Angry Birds
47 Cause for a food recall
49 Advance
51 Yes, in Yokohama
54 Overly inventive . . . or a hint to the answers to 17-, 26- and 42-Across

58 Alan of "Bridge of Spies"
59 Music genre that's sometimes "heavy"
60 Maven
61 Like omega, in the Greek alphabet
62 It's a wrap
63 Big name in oil?

DOWN

1 Drilling grp.
2 Texter's qualifier
3 Third person
4 Muff one
5 Pessimist in Pooh books
6 Online help features, for short
7 "___ in the Morning"
8 Ang who directed "Brokeback Mountain"
9 Double curve
10 Words of encouragement
11 Anarchy queller
12 "This could be bad!"
13 One may be struck
18 Aligns
19 Sweetums
23 "Miss" with regrets
24 "Saturday Night Live" specialty
25 Down Under critters
26 Like the light from distant stars
27 Acquired relative
28 Lies
29 Hardly a celebrity
30 Fauna's counterpart
31 Renaissance Faire weapon
32 Kindle download
37 Is beholden to
38 Pond denizen

40 Singer Lavigne
41 One "hat" for an au pair
43 Many a feline Facebook posting
44 Kind of income a lending officer likes to see
47 List shortcut
48 RC, for one
49 Jared who won an Oscar for "Dallas Buyers Club"
50 Kind of history
51 Carry by semitrailer, say
52 ___ Romeo (Italian car)
53 Doubtful
55 Ambulance letters
56 Farm doc
57 Home for "Girls"

by Adam G. Perl

ACROSS

1 "Goldilocks" bear with the hardest bed
5 Birds that waddle
10 Bridge
14 Wyatt at the O.K. Corral
15 Dickens's ___ Heep
16 Syrup brand used in making pecan pie
17 Is ready for one's star turn, say
20 So-so
21 Exuberance
22 Word accompanying a head slap
23 1992 Tarantino crime thriller
27 Scene not used for the final version of a film
28 Latticework strip
29 Stat for A-Rod or Hammerin' Hank
30 Snow ___ (kids' winter construction)
32 Hangmen's loops
36 Falsetto-voiced Muppet
38 Cookout, briefly . . . or a hint to the ends of 17-, 23-, 52- and 58-Across
40 Fill a position
41 Permeate
44 Bird feeder material
47 Rickey or gimlet ingredient
48 Hearty brews
50 Embarrassed
52 Children of armed forces personnel, slangily
55 Welcome sight?
56 Org. that defends individual rights
57 Bro's sibling
58 Fast, sharp-breaking curveballs
64 Hanker (for)
65 Rimshot instrument
66 Member of an elite Navy team
67 Miso bean

68 Letter-shaped track in metalworking
69 Anything-goes party

DOWN

1 Parishioner's bench
2 Smallish battery
3 8:00–11:00 p.m. on TV
4 H.S. exam graded on a five-point scale
5 Drunk motorist's offense, briefly
6 Decorative vase
7 Oil company with a triangular logo
8 ___ Gibran, author of "The Prophet"
9 Ed with the 2017 #1 hit "Shape of You"
10 Hit the slopes
11 Consumer products giant that makes Tide, for short
12 Mythical 100-eyed giant
13 Snack (on)
18 Bundle of papers
19 Fixated on, as an idea
23 Pound : U.K. :: ___ : Russia
24 "King Kong" and "Citizen Kane" studio
25 Noun go-with
26 Cry before "I know!," in a classroom
27 They're mined and refined
31 Atlanta-based cable inits.
33 Tourist
34 Iroquois foes
35 Email button
37 October birthstone
39 Platform for loading ships
42 Epic poem written in Homeric Greek
43 Bottom-line expense

45 Recede, as the tide
46 Ankle bones
49 Places for mani-pedis
51 Laid down the law
52 National auto body repair chain
53 Like wool on bare skin, typically
54 Neither urban nor suburban
55 Degs. held by Bloomberg and G. W. Bush
59 Mauna ___ (volcano)
60 Sign for a sold-out show
61 Do-over in tennis
62 What an old shirt may be used as
63 Foxy

by Tracy Gray

ACROSS

1 What some castles are made of
5 Goaded (on)
10 Clock setting for an alarm
14 2015 "Rocky" sequel
16 String quartet member
17 Unadorned
18 Honolulu-based carrier, informally
20 Corp. money managers
21 "Big Blue"
22 Like caves with streams running through them
23 Early Uber policy unpopular with drivers
25 "Coke is it!" or "Say 'Pepsi, please'"
27 Piece of pottery featuring Achilles, say
30 Interoffice notes
31 They're heard but not seen
32 Firecracker that goes pfft
33 Money owed
35 Ike's monogram
36 Cut (off)
37 Break . . . such as at the middle of 18-, 27-, 50- or 58-Across?
40 ___ Paulo, Brazil
41 Perch for a ball
42 Humble response to a compliment
43 "___ be my pleasure"
44 "There's something else you should know . . ."
46 Desert refuge
50 Military bottoms, informally
52 How you can shop without leaving home
53 In the thick of
54 Getting close, in a guessing game
56 Trail Blazers' org.
57 Bar mitzvah, e.g.
58 Made snappy comments
62 Meter or liter

63 Rose petal oil
64 Enrique Peña ___, Mexican president beginning in 2012
65 Their maximum scores are 1600
66 Word before "wrong" or "welcome"
67 Bummer

DOWN

1 Serious rift
2 Supportive of cultivation
3 One may attend a class on parenting
4 Antismuggling org.
5 Actress ___ Rachel Wood
6 Tree whose leaves appear in many Chinese fossils
7 ___ long way
8 Certain Ivy Leaguer
9 Utmost, informally
10 "Fresh Off the Boat" network
11 Certain crime boss
12 Stops from slipping
13 Fooled (around)
15 Played some tunes, say
19 McKellen of "The Hobbit"
24 Gives the nod
26 Emphatic rejection
28 Fashion designer Gernreich
29 Says "You and I are done," e.g.
31 Scattered
34 "Fine then!"
36 Unwavering, as a friend
37 "O.K., you got me"
38 Paleo diet staple
39 Tony Stark's alter ego in comics and movies
40 Staying power
43 Mythical figure who flew too close to the sun

44 Special ___ (unconventional missions)
45 "Cross my heart and hope to die!"
47 Baseball pitch that suddenly drops
48 Not quite ready for full release
49 Old salt
51 Clifford who wrote "Golden Boy"
52 Bruin hockey legend
55 Something to build on
59 Japanese figure skater Midori
60 Nickname formed by three consecutive letters of the alphabet
61 El ___ (Spanish hero)

by Michelle Kenney and Jeff Chen

ACROSS

1 Pitchfork-shaped letter
4 Brillo alternative
10 The drug acid, by another name
13 "!!!!," in a text
14 Hairstyling substance
15 Animal whose name is a synonym of "parrot"
16 Kuala Lumpur's locale
19 College teacher, informally
20 "Calvin and Hobbes" conveyance
21 Getting little rainfall
22 Titular California district in a Steinbeck novel
25 Have debts
26 Setting for much of "Moana"
27 Kind of diet regimen based on nonmodern eating habits
30 Dominique ___, 1996 Olympic gymnastics gold medalist
34 "Holy cow!"
35 Hayseed
39 T. J. ___ (department store chain)
40 Arctic bird
41 Counterparts of dots, in Morse code
43 Vinyl albums, for short
44 Issa who stars on HBO's "Insecure"
45 "Fighting" N.C.A.A. team
46 "When they go ___, we go high"
47 4.0, in school
50 Happy accident
51 Shoulder garment
53 Pb, to chemists
54 Not worth discussing
57 Postal delivery
59 California-based gas company
60 Dad
61 "Not guilty," e.g.
62 Hideout
63 "I don't wanna be ___ guy, but . . ."
64 Musk of Tesla
65 Actor Alan
66 Christmas season
67 ___ McNally (mapmaker)

DOWN

1 "___ and Circumstance"
2 Intelligent
3 Ice pad?
4 Person wearing a trench coat and sunglasses, stereotypically
5 Mistake, cutely
6 Odor
7 Group of experts
8 Nike rival
9 Hideout
10 Mrs. George W. Bush
11 Divorced
12 At 0% battery
17 Sporting a natural
18 Deep bow
23 A pair
24 Served dinner
27 Fruit in a fruit basket
28 Contents of el océano
29 1980 Winter Olympics host
31 Washington city with a repetitive name
32 Business fair
33 Annual Austin festival, for short
35 At 50%, to a pessimist
36 ___ of Wight
37 Fashionable
38 University in northeast Ohio
41 N.B.A. star Nowitzki
42 [Alas]
48 Writer Welty
49 Treat really nicely
50 Wild
52 Rest atop
53 With 58-Down, head-in-the-clouds place . . . or a hint to each answer that has four circles
55 Hawaiian island
56 October birthstone
58 See 53-Down

by Erik Agard and Paolo Pasco

ACROSS

1 "___ Don't Lie" (2006 Shakira hit)
5 Fund
10 Ruler deposed in 1979
14 Father of Ahab in the Bible
15 Composer whose name is Italian for "green"
16 Sharpen, as a skill
17 1,001 causes of anxiety?
19 "___ baby!"
20 Doc who might perform laryngologic surgery
21 ___ Enterprise
22 Spotted
24 Gives kudos to
26 101 rear ends?
28 "Darn it!"
30 "___ the next"
31 Inseparable
32 ___ noire (pet peeve)
33 Poke
35 Charged toward
37 51 cats?
40 Twitch
43 Makeup smearer
44 Like a long shot's chances
48 Singer Garfunkel
49 Frost
51 Strangely repulsive sort
53 Six members of a "Dallas" family?
55 Provo resident
56 Fly
57 Poke
59 ___-wop
60 Ibsen's "Peer ___"
61 501 renditions?
65 Suffix with kitchen
66 Clearing in the woods

67 Hike along the Appalachian Trail, e.g.
68 Way in or way out
69 Designer Perry
70 He loved Lucy

DOWN

1 Many a meth production site
2 "That was . . . amazing!"
3 Cheap way to get media attention
4 Convene, as a legislature
5 Two big nights in December
6 Loch ___
7 H.M.O. V.I.P.s
8 Wordsworth work
9 Most sensible
10 You might run to get in it
11 Branding tool
12 Insect feeler
13 Telemarketer's accessory
18 Deteriorate with inactivity
23 Squirrel away
25 Pacers' engagements?
26 Picnic items
27 World's most populous democracy
29 Beach bottle letters
34 Adjust the price on
36 It's no liability
38 Paintballer's cry
39 Org. concerned with meltdowns

40 Criticized brutally
41 In on
42 Eroded
45 Galena or cerussite
46 Devices with Siri
47 Relative of a snowboard
50 Tense
52 Summons a genie, perhaps
54 Word repeated before "everywhere"
57 Yoda, e.g.
58 Son of Zeus
62 Kind of wind that blows no good
63 Actor Kilmer of "Tombstone"
64 "___ be my pleasure"

by Bruce Haight

ACROSS

1 The Times or the Daily News, e.g.
6 Gorillas
10 Mark permanently
14 Ogden Nash's "two-l" beast
15 Seized car, for short
16 You, in the Bible
17 ___ nerve (retina attachment)
18 Guitarist Clapton
19 Chopped
20 Visibly tense
23 ___ Paulo, Brazil
24 Crucial biological molecule
25 Figure in Greek myth after whom a continent is named
28 Compete (for)
29 ___ and starts
31 Opposite of oui
32 Extremely jealous
36 Characteristic
38 Convent residents
39 Rich ore sources
41 Counterpart to "if," in computer science
42 Aids in crime
44 In the very act
46 Lancelot's title
47 Highest point
49 Qty.
50 Truss up
52 Letters before a pseudonym
53 Golf teacher
56 Deplorably cowardly
60 Spheres
62 Holder of a cafeteria meal
63 Like some wealthy neighborhoods
64 In apple-pie order
65 Things in an Easter basket
66 In the slightest
67 Agile for one's age

68 Supplies for Easter 65-Across
69 Antonym of 64-Across

DOWN

1 Snow clearers
2 Start or end of the Greek spelling of "Athena"
3 Place between a house and a backyard
4 Give off, as rays
5 Entered quickly
6 Place of gladiatorial battle
7 Lima's land
8 Three-hour-plus movie, maybe
9 Holder of an eye or a light bulb
10 Heavens, poetically
11 Ex of Marla and Ivana, informally
12 Dairy animal
13 Attila, for one
21 Prepare to be knighted
22 One of the seven deadly sins
26 Graceful bearing
27 Threw some chips in the pot
28 Item under a suit jacket
29 Company that bought Kinko's
30 Picked out of a lineup, informally
32 Grind, as the teeth
33 Florida senator Marco
34 Snack for an athlete
35 Times long, long ago

37 $250, for Mediterranean Avenue, even with a hotel on it
40 Ice cream drink
43 Go yachting
45 Blend
48 Bombarded, as with snowballs
51 Irritable
52 Bottomless pit
53 Breads served with hummus
54 Staggers
55 "Strangely enough . . ."
57 Unrestrained revelry
58 Salary
59 Running behind schedule
60 Walk-___ (unrecruited athletes)
61 Member of Cong.

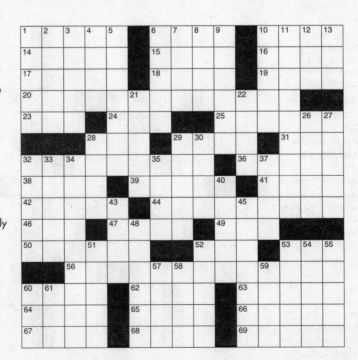

by Tom McCoy

ACROSS

1 Tacks on
5 Not include
9 Had fingers crossed
14 Front of a freighter
15 Duffer's warning
16 + end on an electrolytic cell
17 Birdbath organism
18 Bushy dos
19 Vegetation along a British golf course
20 Yard displays at election time
23 Color tone
24 Org. for the Big East, Big South and Big 12
25 Family tree members
28 Geologist's division
29 Mongol Empire founder
31 "Gymnopédies" composer Erik
33 Geologist's division
34 Claudius's successor
35 Small amount
38 ___-Ball
40 Yea or nay
43 Goat's bleat
45 Stops playing
49 "Nope, guess again"
53 Cracklin' ___ Bran
54 Susan who wrote "In America"
55 U.S. city whose name looks oxymoronic
56 Lead-in to an alias
57 Nonactive member of a firm . . . or what G, H and W each have in 20-, 29- and 49-Across?
60 Sharp increase
62 Burnett of CNN
63 It'll give you a clear picture
64 K. T. of country music
65 Offer mortgages
66 "That makes sense"
67 Trattoria course
68 Staying power, informally
69 George Foreman Jr., George Foreman III, George Foreman IV, etc.

DOWN

1 Army fliers since 1984
2 Advice-giver on SiriusXM
3 Serving in Asia that's taboo in the West
4 Exchange
5 Setting for "Dilbert"
6 New York's ___ Library
7 Period in Europe starting around 1100 B.C.
8 "___ of the D'Urbervilles"
9 Sheep dish popular in Scotland
10 Preparing to propose, by tradition
11 Boxster maker
12 Mag. staffers
13 Actor Billy ___ Williams
21 Ire
22 Unerasably, say
26 Body part that some people wiggle
27 ___ Balls (snack food)
30 Sounds from the Jolly Green Giant
32 Aid in producing a suspect's picture
36 Picture
37 Test ___ (treaty subject)
39 Blunder
40 Bugs on the road?
41 Medalla de ___ (first-place award in Mexico)
42 Painful things to have removed
44 Source of wood for baseball bats
46 Scoundrel
47 Break during rehearsal, say
48 Doesn't eat for a long while
50 Main ore of lead
51 Erasing, as a hard drive
52 African antelopes
58 "Little" Dickens girl
59 "___ is the life!"
60 Soak up
61 Smokey Bear was in an early one, for short

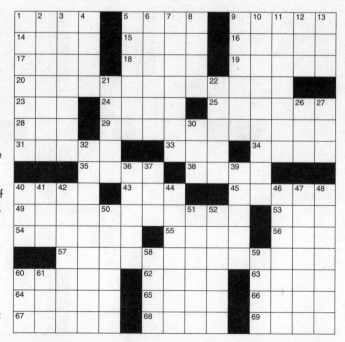

by Don Gagliardo and Zhouqin Burnikel

ACROSS

1 Puff ___ (snake)
6 Bit of Brylcreem, say
9 Following
14 Prince Harry's mum
15 It hatches from a big egg
16 Unmanned aircraft
17 With 3-Down, useful
18 ___ Keane, "The Family Circus" cartoonist
19 With 11-Down, snobbish
20 California's old Fort ___
21 Soupy "Oliver Twist" fare
23 Cosmetician Lauder
24 Award named for the winningest pitcher of all time
26 Ones sacrificing for a cause
28 Santa ___ winds
29 Firm (up), as muscles
30 Long, hard journeys
33 Old coupon for the needy
38 Greeting from a parade float
39 With 29-Down, sophisticated
40 Listening device on a narc
41 Realtor's showing
43 Murdered
44 Grand Ole ___
45 Put on, as a TV show
46 Patron of France
50 Produces a large body of work?
54 "It is my desire . . ."
55 Word that can follow sea, solar or staying
57 "How relaxing!"
58 With 48-Down, affectionate
59 Part of the Freudian psyche

60 With 51-Down, weak and indecisive
62 Trapped on a branch
63 Screw things up
64 Walk leisurely
65 Authority
66 Man cave, maybe
67 Crust, mantle or core, for the earth

DOWN

1 ___ committee
2 Book that might require a key to open
3 See 17-Across
4 Finish
5 Sci-fi weapons
6 Fix, as software
7 French female friend
8 Symbol of Teddy Roosevelt's political party
9 Sticks (to)

10 Ice, as a cake
11 See 19-Across
12 Go inside
13 Spanish kings
22 Genetic initials
25 Like some wooden buckets
27 Roddick or Rooney
29 See 39-Across
30 What it takes to tango
31 Genre for Big Sean or Biggie Smalls
32 She raised Cain
33 Like most manual transmissions in the 1970s and '80s
34 Spin, as a baton
35 First-___ kit
36 CT scan alternative
37 It's "mightier than the sword"
39 Arizona tribe

42 ___ list (tasks for one's spouse)
43 Active during the daytime
45 Card that beats a king
46 River deposits
47 ___ Birch, "American Beauty" actress
48 See 58-Across
49 Fencing blades
50 Bound by an oath
51 See 60-Across
52 Ping-Pong surface
53 More timid
56 Grotesque folklore figure
61 Org. for docs

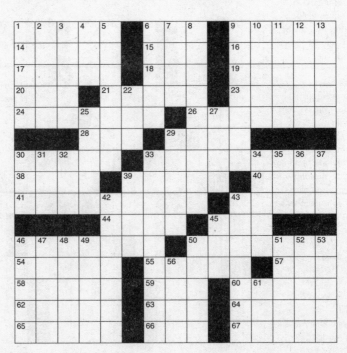

by Bruce Haight

ACROSS

1 Fruity soft drink
5 Stir-fry cookers
9 Puts into English, say, as movie dialogue
13 Schiff on the House Intelligence Committee
14 Things teeth and hair have
16 Rights org. of which Helen Keller was a co-founder
17 Comedian Kevin after having a sloppy jelly snack?
19 Writer Lowry with two Newbery Medals
20 Restaurateur Paula
21 Lion observed at night
22 Naysaying
23 Fashion flair
25 Get frisky with comedian Freddie?
27 Intricate trap
28 Azure expanse
30 Mule in an Erie Canal song
31 School for young royals
33 Irritating criticism
36 "The Phantom of the Opera" city
40 Comedian Richard being sent to a psychiatric facility?
43 Sample
44 Swimmer Diana
45 Away on a submarine, say
46 "___ the fields we go . . ."
48 Séance sound
50 Blubber
51 Cause of comedian Roseanne's black eye?
56 Touches geographically
58 "Superfood" Amazon berry
59 Captain Hook, to Peter Pan
60 Big unicycle part
61 Sulk
62 Result of comedian Eric's untied shoelaces?

66 Subject of Queen Elizabeth, informally
67 John le Carré heroes
68 Timely benefit
69 "500" race, familiarly
70 Take one's leave
71 Breakfast brand for the toaster

DOWN

1 Forty winks
2 Prof's URL ender
3 Robust-sounding teens of children's books
4 Incite to action
5 St. Paul's Cathedral architect
6 "Would you look at that!"
7 Nocturnal marsupial
8 Scatter
9 Spiritual leader with a Nobel Peace Prize
10 NE basketball powerhouse
11 Football rush
12 Essman of "Curb Your Enthusiasm"
15 Comes to a standstill
18 Alternative to Levi's
23 Took the entire series
24 Colorful aquarium fish
25 Tall supporting tower
26 Totally captivated
29 "Finger-lickin' good" food establishment
32 Achievement for Bernie Madoff or Al Capone
34 Youngest of the fictional March sisters
35 "Attention ___ shoppers!"
37 St. Bernard during an avalanche, maybe
38 Chemically nonreactive
39 Remains
41 Coral formation
42 Hollywood's Lupino

47 Repeated jazz phrases
49 Big nuisance
51 Thumper's deer friend
52 Tidbit for a squirrel
53 Quick
54 What Tarzan's friends advised him to do?
55 Half of a genetic molecule
57 Illegal payment
60 Trial balloon
63 Hawaiian gift
64 Fireplace item
65 Ambient musician Brian

by Joy Behar and Lynn Lempel

ACROSS

1 Salmon or sole
5 Somersault
9 Rough on the eyes or ears
14 "Fancy seeing you here!"
15 Ages and ages
16 The same
17 Chicken pen
18 A B C D E F G
20 Fitting
21 Merriment
22 Longtime Time magazine rival, briefly
23 A B C D F
27 Opposite of 'neath
28 Slippery 1-Across
29 Hay storage areas
33 Plan that's "hatched"
36 Campbell's container
38 Narrow inlet
39 B C F H I K N O P S U V W Y
43 Have a bug, maybe
44 French affirmative
45 Stops
46 Bundles of hay
49 Strands in a cell?
51 Not the main choice: Abbr.
52 G R X
57 Taj Mahal material
60 "My Country, ___ of Thee"
61 Glass of "This American Life"
62 A B O
65 Jump in an ice rink
66 Cottage or cabin
67 ___ of Sandwich
68 Gardening tools
69 Lecherous figure of myth
70 Eye affliction
71 Paul who sang "Eso Beso"

DOWN

1 Centrally located
2 "Fingers crossed!"
3 Utterly ruined, informally
4 Cool
5 Longest and strongest bone in the human body
6 Take it easy
7 Drop-___ (surprise visitors)
8 It comes between chi and omega
9 Fairy tale character who leaves a trail of bread crumbs in the forest
10 King of Naples in "The Tempest"
11 Bar mitzvah or communion
12 Distort, as data
13 Gas company famous for its toy trucks
19 Cow's chew
21 Physicist Enrico
24 Swarm (with)
25 Lie back
26 "Sad to say . . ."
30 Play and film about a 1977 series of interviews with a former president
31 One of a hundred in Scrabble
32 Impudence
33 Sign of healing
34 ___ Pet (1980s fad item)
35 Prefix with conscious or freak
37 Big Apple inits.
40 Car with the slogan "Truth in engineering"
41 Butcher's offerings
42 East Indies tourist destination
47 Exemplify
48 Electrician's alloy
50 Major highway
53 One who's back from war, informally
54 Bridal path
55 "It's all ___ to me"
56 Spicy dance or dip
57 Some Wharton degs.
58 Jessica of "Sin City"
59 Yam or turnip
63 Affirmative
64 Reassuring touch
65 Cry upon getting a tough crossword clue

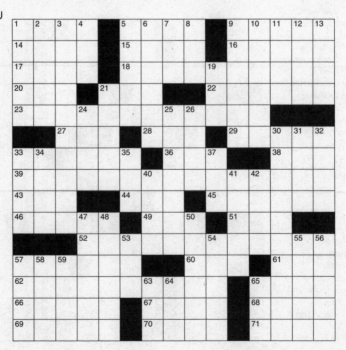

by Trenton Charlson

ACROSS

1 River to the Caspian Sea
6 Speedy
11 ___ the line (obey)
14 Like some walls at Harvard
15 Tureen dipper
16 Humble dwelling
17 One might stare at the Sun
19 Suffix in many ore names
20 Paris's ___ Palace
21 Submarine sandwich meat
22 Linux forerunner
23 It holds four pecks
26 NBC host Carson
29 1986–2001 Earth orbiter
30 Outback flock
31 Prefix with sex or cycle
32 Banco de México money
33 Retort to a doubter
36 With 38-Across, feature of an upscale kitchen . . . or of 17-, 23-, 47- and 58-Across?
38 See 36-Across
39 Message that might start with "@"
40 Whitney and Shasta, for two: Abbr.
42 "To Kill a Mockingbird" author
43 Former piece of an ice shelf
45 Affirmative in "Fargo"
46 Huskies' haul
47 Manager at a train depot
51 What an insole helps support
52 Darlin'
53 Julius who sang "Anywhere I Wander," 1953

57 [Har har!]
58 Discussions that might lead to a treaty
60 Master pilot
61 Capital of Jordan
62 Wiped out big-time
63 ___ Royal Highness
64 Moist-eyed
65 Catch at a rodeo

DOWN

1 A shady person may give off a bad one
2 Track shape
3 Water ___ (pond plant)
4 Subsists
5 Parting word that's 80% vowels
6 ___-mo
7 Medal of Honor recipient
8 Something to strive for
9 Served in blazing liquor
10 .
11 Set one's sights low
12 Tummy protrusion
13 Writing in digital format
18 Famed German hypnotist
22 Bar habitué's order, with "the"
24 ___ Royal Highness
25 Slightly off
26 Channel for fumes
27 All over again
28 Player who might tackle a wide receiver
32 Kind of dish at a lab
34 Old-fashioned dagger
35 Had too much, briefly
37 Places for crowns
38 Really suffering, so to speak
40 Neighbor of Bangladesh
41 Touch in baseball
44 "Leave!"
46 Rock bands?
47 "Open wide!"
48 Cease-fire
49 "Psycho" mother
50 Birth-related
54 Plaza de toros cries
55 Tackles a black diamond trail, say
56 Concerning
58 Liposculpture target
59 "With ___ luck . . ."

by Chuck Deodene

68

ACROSS

1 Civil rights pioneer Du Bois
4 Shade of blue
8 Rant
14 Chicago's home: Abbr.
15 Racer with the tortoise
16 Like a show with a single performer
17 Only major-league player to enter the 3,000-hit club in the 1980s
19 Ranting
20 1965 Beatles hit that starts "Ooh, I need your love, babe"
22 Donkey
23 Final bubble on a questionnaire, maybe
24 Something a barber has to work around
26 Maidenform product
27 Catch, as on a thorn
31 HBO show hosted by John Oliver
36 And so on: Abbr.
37 Home for the Hawks and Braves: Abbr.
38 Equal: Prefix
39 Pal of Pooh
40 1974 John Updike novel
44 Greek cheese
45 Winery container
46 Verbal stumbles
47 Tattoo artist
50 Bug spray brand
52 The change from Julian to Gregorian . . . or what would be needed to make 20-, 31- and 40-Across possible?
58 A snake has a forked one
59 Engages in military conflict
60 Acting grown-up
61 Barely
62 Three on a grandfather clock
63 Dictation experts
64 Hankerings
65 Newspaper staffers, for short

DOWN

1 Electronic money transfer
2 "The Time Machine" people
3 Edifice: Abbr.
4 Informal talks
5 Gridiron gains
6 Bay ___ (San Francisco, Oakland, etc.)
7 When repeated, Frank Sinatra title city
8 Holy Jewish scroll
9 Wowed
10 Classic game with black-and-white discs
11 Female friend for François
12 Cold and damp, as a dungeon
13 Main lang. of the Commonwealth countries
18 Nautical map
21 Believer in a strong federal government
24 Message on a cake in "Alice in Wonderland"
25 Fancy tie
26 Pulitzer-winning Toni Morrison novel
28 Google ___ Viewer (tool for charting word frequency over time)
29 Ship-to-ship communications?
30 Classic Pontiacs
31 Flip (through)
32 Angkor ___ (Cambodian site)
33 Biblical verb suffix
34 The Beavers of the Pac-12, for short
35 The "N" of NCO
41 Carpenter's tool that's faster than a hammer
42 Very distant
43 Homer Simpson's favorite beers
48 Prefix with science
49 Crawling on hands and ___
50 Church instrument
51 Supplies with meals
52 Jacket
53 Upfront bet
54 Give stars to
55 Little injury, in baby talk
56 Antipest spray
57 Some hospital pics
58 Things with ® symbols: Abbr.

by Joe Deeney

ACROSS

1 "___: Ragnarok" (2017 Marvel film)
5 Give new weapons to
10 This, on the periodic table
14 Dream: Fr.
15 Grain disease
16 1967 Montreal event
17 Specks in la mer
18 This, on the periodic table
19 Carefully examines
20 Evacuation notice?
22 Ventura who was governor of Minnesota
23 Hungers (for)
24 You might lose yours in an argument
26 911 responder, for short
27 Gourmet food additive
29 Lout
32 Highest point
34 Place to buy tickets: Abbr.
35 Medical research goal
36 This, on the periodic table
39 Passed, as a law
41 Gets into the weeds?
42 One might be around a buck or two
44 Canadian gas brand
45 End of the British alphabet
46 Perish alternative
48 Abbr. in an email header
51 Sent astray
52 Person making introductions
54 This, on the periodic table
57 Opaque liquids such as milk
59 Minnesota's ___ Clinic
60 Ticket ___
61 Modern prefix with complete or correct
62 Well-matched
63 Au pair, often
64 Turkey ___ (annual event)
65 Makes after taxes
66 Fur trader John Jacob
67 What "This" refers to, in this puzzle's theme: Abbr.

DOWN

1 Unimportant thing
2 This, on the periodic table
3 Wore out, as one's welcome
4 Bowling alley button
5 Not made up
6 Printing goofs
7 Act hostilely
8 Apartment sharer
9 Denali, e.g.: Abbr.
10 "When pigs fly!"
11 Opponents in custody cases
12 Picks, with "for"
13 Elephant's trunk, basically
21 Balance sheet plus
22 With 25-Down, 727 and 747
25 See 22-Down
28 Book that describes the crossing of the Red Sea
29 How some legal disputes get settled
30 "The British ___ coming!"
31 Stuck coins into
33 Additional afterthought, for short
35 Includes when sending an email
36 Radio freq. unit
37 Wade's opponent in legal history
38 The answer to each clue that says "This, on the periodic table"
40 BBQ leftovers?
43 The answer to each clue that says "This, on the periodic table"
46 Wrestling win
47 "Uh, no idea"
49 Continued talking
50 Mississippi River explorer
51 Blue Lucky Charms marshmallows
53 Mazda roadster
54 Superhero group including Beast and Cyclops
55 Icicle's place
56 Kremlin rejection
58 Astronomer's unit: Abbr.
60 Southern California's Santa ___ Freeway

by Mark MacLachlan

ACROSS

1 Fancy neckwear
6 "Zip your lip!"
10 Something that might be said with fingers crossed behind the back
13 Classroom item that spins
14 Kind of diet replicating that of early humans
15 Wedding vow
16 It must be removed before pouring coolant into an engine
18 Writer Tolstoy
19 Bedazzle
20 Lower's opposite
21 Unkind
22 Elizabeth II's home outside London
26 Hand drum
27 Secreted
28 Quaint train amenity
32 Churchill Downs event
36 Ye ___ Shoppe
37 Less outgoing
39 Big wind
40 Documents shown at border checkpoints
42 Feline that doesn't stray
44 Test for seekers of a 21-Down, for short
46 Sugary
47 Where rum and rye may be stored
53 Feverish chills
54 Nerve
55 Fink
58 ___-de-France
59 Creature found "swimming" in 16-, 22-, 28-, 42- and 47-Across
62 ___ v. Wade
63 Maze marking next to an arrow
64 Show host
65 ___ of a gun

66 Famed loch
67 Penguin or T. rex in the modern version of Monopoly

DOWN

1 Taj Mahal city
2 BBQ side dish
3 Substitute terms for sensitive subjects
4 Kimono tie
5 Afternoon repast
6 Marx brother who never spoke
7 Stomach trouble
8 Google.com function
9 Partner of skip and jump
10 Serving of sole
11 Like a five-star Yelp review
12 Frontiersman Daniel
14 Bursts, as a balloon

17 Elizabeth I was the last of them
21 Common grad sch. credential
23 Joined (with)
24 Doctors Without Borders, e.g., in brief
25 What Doctors Without Borders provides
26 "___ Ha'i" ("South Pacific" song)
28 Long-running PBS film series
29 Home of the Cubs, for short
30 Firebrand Rand
31 Color in sunsets
33 Churchill Downs, e.g.
34 Trombone honk, e.g.
35 "Are we there ___?"
38 More optimistic
41 Sold-out box-office sign

43 The "O" of B.Y.O.B.
45 Valuable white fur
47 Bears' retreats
48 Probably not a summer home
49 "Bohemian Rhapsody" band
50 Indianapolis team
51 Highway tolls may be based on the number of them
52 Casket stand
56 Away from the wind
57 One under 20
59 Documentarian Burns
60 Sopping ___
61 Wellness grp.

by Jennifer Nutt

ACROSS

1 Flaky mineral
5 She "walked like a woman and talked like a man," in a Kinks song
9 Say with conviction
13 Lots
14 Film format that's sometimes in 3-D
15 Mushroom's reproductive cell
16 Refined chap
17 Base for long-distance carriers?
19 "This is looking extremely bad for me!"
21 Person setting the stage?
22 Archaeologist played by Harrison Ford, informally
23 Lyricist Gershwin
25 Ricky Martin's "Livin' La Vida ___"
26 South Asian shade tree
28 Prohibit
29 Fuel that contributes to global warming
30 A mere pittance
33 What "X" might represent on a treasure map
34 An official language of Canada: Abbr.
35 Ink-squirting creature
40 Unexpected hit
43 Size in a lingerie shop
47 Rebel on many T-shirts
48 Wears away
49 ". . . ish"
50 "The Star-Spangled Banner" contraction
51 Hardly an upscale bar
52 Cell that fires on impulse
54 Emission from radioactive decay
57 Cleopatra's lover

60 Shower affection (on)
61 Annual athletic awards
62 Canadian Plains tribe
63 Wee bit
64 Eliot who chased Capone
65 File size units, informally
66 IDs collected by H.R.

DOWN

1 Storied traveling trio
2 Unit in an online cart
3 "I'm listening . . ."
4 Stop and go, e.g.
5 "Sing" without singing
6 Leave out
7 Fall behind
8 Body spray brand
9 High-level H.S. class with integrals
10 It has its charms

11 Beethoven's Third
12 Undo, as a law
15 ___-Cat (winter vehicle)
18 Chimp's relative
20 Grows fur for the winter, say
23 Pro at building financial worth, slangily
24 Kitchen appliance
26 Secretive email option
27 "That's the spot!"
31 Actress Anne of "Donnie Brasco"
32 ___ de corps
36 1951 film featuring Nero
37 Brand of kids' wear with Superman and Batman options
38 Filler for a cooler
39 Some A.L. sluggers

41 N.C.A.A. women's basketball powerhouse
42 Overnight flights
43 People who target the starts of 17-, 30-, 40- and 57-Across
44 Paper fold
45 Takes by force
46 Raunchy 1981 comedy with two sequels
53 Intl. group headquartered in D.C.
54 Rare blood type, for short
55 Memo heading abbr.
56 Pro votes
58 Channel showing old films
59 Valuable rock

by Jeff Chen

ACROSS

1 Online source of film trivia
5 When doubled, a Hawaiian fish
9 A lot
14 Sour expression
15 "Yeah, right!"
16 Give permission
17 Period dominated by the likes of Dan Rather and Peter Jennings?
19 Stop competing as an amateur
20 Like dry, clumpy mud
21 Cool, in '90s slang
23 Blacken, as by fire
24 Joan who sang at Woodstock
26 Period when every car was a junker?
28 Hairless
30 Boise's state: Abbr.
32 Dawn goddess
33 Painful boo-boo
34 English-speaking neighbor of Venezuela
36 Maple syrup source
39 Period known for its 007 movies?
41 Period of fuzzy sweaters?
43 So last year
44 Swallowed quickly
46 Classic Diana Ross hairdo
47 Strategy-free card game
48 Wedding vow
49 Gradually remove, as from a mother's milk
50 Period when tribute bands thrived?
54 Flees
56 Go wild in the streets
57 Reason to pull an all-nighter
59 Backs of necks
62 "I was with my mistress at the time," maybe
64 Period when psychiatrists ruled?
66 Cross-dressing Disney heroine of 1998
67 Chimney buildup
68 Supply-and-demand subj.
69 Fire starter
70 Chooses
71 The first "R" of R&R

DOWN

1 Apple introduction of 1998
2 "___ Lisa"
3 Hunter's hiding spot in a marsh
4 Guillotined
5 Tarnish or deface
6 "Right away!"
7 Turnpike, e.g.
8 Lead-in to bad news
9 Droop
10 Things seen in most public buildings, but almost never in casinos
11 A, as in Aristotle
12 Kerchief worn as headgear
13 Used foul language
18 Keats poem
22 Elvis in the 1950s or Justin Bieber in the 2010s
25 Stepped tower of ancient Sumer
27 Anthracite, e.g.
28 Classic clown with a repetitive name
29 Missing, as a G.I.
31 Climax of "Hamilton"
35 Mimicked
36 Campus sanctuary, in modern parlance
37 Taj Mahal locale
38 Lowly worker
40 Food-thickening agent
42 Legislator
45 Specialty bakery
47 Home mixology station
50 Pulls an all-nighter, say
51 Prepare for a bodybuilding contest
52 "And there it is!"
53 Painting surface
55 ___ Arbor, Mich.
58 Gait between a walk and a canter
60 Causes of bigheadedness
61 Mailed
63 What quills are dipped in
65 "___ Always Sunny in Philadelphia"

by Timothy Polin

ACROSS

1 One of the Five Pillars of Islam
5 Shakespeare, informally
9 Mists
15 "Interesting . . ."
16 Spark, so to speak
17 Taiwan's capital
18 *"You fail to understand what I'm saying"
21 Nursery purchase
22 Smidgen
23 Info for a driver at an airport
24 *Cheesy fare served at a bar?
29 Old Renault
31 Berry marketed as healthful
32 Chaplin of "Game of Thrones"
33 Sanctify
34 Island garland
35 Bowled over
36 12-time Vatican name
38 *2006 cult-classic action film
43 Flubs
44 Hurdle for a Ph.D. candidate, typically
45 Firefighter's tool
47 One-named Spanish-born actress
50 No longer mint
51 Gush
52 Get connected after typing one's password
53 *"This relationship is smothering me"
55 Conjunction in the middle of a famous palindrome
56 Vegetable with pods
58 Narrow inlet
59 What a sci-fi portal might lead to . . . or what's added successively to the ends of the answers to the starred clues

66 "The Bathers" painter
67 Symphony, e.g.
68 Spicy chocolate sauce
69 Trample
70 Horses that could be hounds or badgers?
71 Took to court

DOWN

1 Box-office success
2 Pale wood
3 Org. in "Breaking Bad"
4 Lakeside rental
5 Energy source from a "farm"
6 Swear words?
7 Permit to
8 Eva Mendes or Eva Longoria
9 Editor's override
10 Official decree from the Vatican
11 2016 Olympics city, informally
12 Each
13 Busybodies
14 Musical instruments with frets
19 Trifling amount
20 Tough row to ___
24 Bud
25 Finishes, as a cake
26 Genesis son
27 Loamy soil
28 Intro to Chinese?
30 "Frozen" princess
35 LeBron James's hometown
36 "Gay" capital
37 Certain network ID
39 Streamlined, for short
40 Missing part of the Sphinx
41 Mecca for oenophiles
42 "Suit"

46 Source of feta cheese
47 Unclogs
48 Big buzzer
49 Early toddlerhood
50 Japanese eel-and-rice dish
51 Involuntary jerks
53 Like the verbs "lie" and "lay": Abbr.
54 Do wrong
57 Jerome who composed "Ol' Man River"
60 Blouse or sweater
61 Hoppy quaff, for short
62 Container for a 61-Down
63 Marker letters
64 Soccer match shout
65 Mustachioed character on "The Simpsons"

by Damon Gulczynski

ACROSS

1 Burden of proof
5 "Like ___" (remark dismissing concern)
10 Tried to steal second, maybe
14 Impudent
15 Things called in roll call
16 French film
17 "Look how great I did!"
18 Computer help for a witch?
20 Fish that's a source of caviar
22 Smooth transition from one topic to the next
23 Gradually withdraw, as from the bottle
24 Wearing only a bottom
26 Educational institution for witches?
29 Clock sound at 6 a.m., maybe
30 Engrossed
31 Centerpiece of a beer bash
34 Canines
35 Aches and ___
37 Possess
38 Takes too much, briefly
39 Tempo
40 Like a haunted house
41 How one might be forced to accept a witch?
44 Japanese warrior
47 "The Ghost and Mrs. ___" (1947 movie)
48 Super tennis servers
49 July 4, for the United States
53 Utterances from witches?
56 Dublin's land
57 Lit ___ (coll. course)
58 Seriously overweight
59 Similar (to)
60 Grains used in Cheerios
61 "Hyperion" poet John
62 Wines like Beaujolais and Chianti

DOWN

1 Chooses (to)
2 Tidy
3 Language of Pakistan
4 Sci-fi movie that's inspired many a Halloween costume
5 Line down a pant leg
6 Chickens for roasting
7 "I'll second that!"
8 Seminary subj.
9 Immigrant's subj.
10 Actor Maximilian
11 Feudal lord
12 Ear bone
13 Hockey feints
19 Bill worth 100 smackers
21 Target for a disinfectant wipe
24 Hotter ___ hell
25 "My bad!"
26 Dirt clump
27 Witches
28 Moans and groans, e.g.
29 "Much ___ About Nothing"
31 Marx who co-wrote "The Communist Manifesto"
32 Like Michael Myers of "Halloween"
33 "Huh, fancy that!"
35 Prefix with legal or trooper
36 Start of a play
37 "I'll second that!"
39 Analyze grammatically
40 Rearrange, as text
41 German sausages
42 In the thick of
43 Ones patient with patients
44 Vanzetti's partner in 1920s crime
45 Honda luxury brand
46 Kind of badge for a boy scout
49 La ___ Tar Pits
50 Construction on the coast of Holland
51 Lacking rainfall
52 Hankerings
54 Stir-fry vessel
55 U.K. award

by Jay Kaskel

ACROSS

1 With 65-Across, author of the "Ninety-Five Theses," posted on 10/31/1517
7 Leatherworker's tool
10 Numbers on a golf course
14 Each
15 Tell a tall tale
16 Home of Zion National Park
17 With 24-Across, movement resulting from the "Ninety-Five Theses"
19 Flight board info
20 Lo-fat
21 Not wild
22 Intrinsically
23 Ernie of the World Golf Hall of Fame
24 See 17-Across
26 Contents of a bog
27 Pet food brand
28 Muslim woman's head covering
31 ___ Lingus
32 Breakfast bar bits
36 Building where the "Ninety-Five Theses" were posted
40 Boxing stats
41 Bambi's mother, for one
42 Genre for the "Pokémon" series
43 What sac flies produce
45 Whole bunch
47 Practice condemned in the "Ninety-Five Theses"
51 Distant
54 Give a leg up
55 Part of the 36-Across where the "Ninety-Five Theses" were posted
56 ___ Korbut, 1970s Olympic gymnastics star
57 [Ugh, here we go again]
58 City where the "Ninety-Five Theses" were written
60 J. D. Salinger title character
61 "___ Maria" (hymn)
62 "It's all clear to me now!"
63 Not distant
64 "With pleasure!"
65 See 1-Across

DOWN

1 Kind of syrup
2 Easter's month, usually
3 Runs amok
4 French bean?
5 Freezer buildup
6 Lipton rival
7 "Remember the ___!"
8 Many Napa establishments
9 Give permission to
10 Body of water bordering Seattle
11 Company that made Pong
12 "Midnight Cowboy" role
13 Charlie of "Two and a Half Men"
18 Only U.S. president also to serve as chief justice
22 Cooking spray brand
24 Singer McEntire
25 Painter Chagall
26 Sack seeker
28 Bowler or boater
29 Type
30 Self-titled #1 pop album of 2001
31 Cleaned the dishes?
33 NPR host Shapiro
34 Channel with an annual month-long Oscar celebration
35 "That's all ___ wrote"
37 "That's cool with me!"
38 Plummet
39 Actor Lukas of "Witness"
44 Three-layer sandwich, for short
45 Person whose name might start with Mc-
46 Post production?
47 "Hedda Gabler" playwright
48 Static, e.g.
49 Something taken on faith
50 Memos
51 Edible part of a fruit
52 Concur
53 Wild party, in slang
56 Newspaper piece that always starts at the end?
58 Course of action
59 Madame ___ of 1960s Vietnam

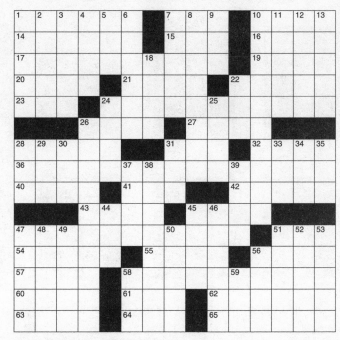

by Alex Eaton-Salners

The New York Times

SMART PUZZLES

Presented with Style

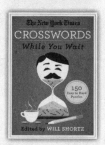

Available at your local bookstore or online at www.nytimes.com/nytstore

🦊 St. Martin's Griffin

1

```
O L A V . O F A R T . S H A H
S O L O . N I M E S . C O S A
H A L L O F F A M E . A N T I
A T F . G O T T O . C L E R K
. H E L L O H O W A R E Y O U
. M O E T . . B U D . . . . .
O P A L . S T R U M . R E P .
H I L L S T R E E T B L U E S
O N E . T H I E F . . E L L A
. . A A A . . P A N E . . . .
H O L L Y W O O D A C T O R .
A R E A S . V I O L A . F I R
S I R S . H U L L A B A L O O
T O O K . S L E E T . B A J A
E N Y A . T E R S E . S W A N
```

2

```
A I D S . P L U S . I T E M S
R O U E . R A P T . N A S A L
T W E E H O U S E . S U P R A
S A L S A . R E A M . G R I T
. . . . S W A T M A C H I N E
O A K L E Y . . R U T T E D .
W H I S K E Y M O V E . . . .
L A N D . E O E . B A R S . .
. . . W O W E D M O U T H S .
S A M S O N . A W G O O N . .
Q U A C K O F D A W N . . . .
U S N A . R E A D . E M C E E
A S T R A . E L M E R F U D D
S I R E N . L A I R . A B I G
H E A D Y . S I N E . S A T E
```

3

```
D A W N . S T A N . A L O F T
A G R O . A R I A . R A Z O R
R O O S E V E L T . A M O R E
I N T E R I M . O R G A N D Y
N Y E . R O O T . H O S E . .
. . H A R R I S O N . H O P .
C O M E T S . M A S . W O R E
O B A M A . D O G . T Y L E R
P I C S . J O T . E R N E S T
E T A . B U C H A N A N . . .
. D A R N . Y E L L . P R E .
S T A T I O N . N I E L S E N
H A M I D . C L E V E L A N D
E F I L E . A T I E . C L E O
S T A T S . A D D N . S M E W
```

4

```
A G A V E S . S P A . A L L A
I O M O T H . E D U . T E A R
D R Y I C E . A F R O P I C K
A P P L E P I E . A R R A Y S
. . O A T . L E S S E E . . .
I V E . C E L L O . L S A T S
D O H A . A S S T . S E T U P
E L L I O T . K E N O B I . .
S T E R N . P T U I . T M E N
T A R P S . R U S T S . I D S
. . I P H O N E . O T C . . .
D C A R E A . A R T P A P E R
A L P A C I N O . O S C I N E
F O O T . K O I . G U I L D S
T Y P E . U R L . A P T E S T
```

5

```
C A N D O . L I M A . E P P S
B L E A K . A P O P . A L O E
S T A R E S D O W N . T A P E
. A T T E N D S . E A S I E R
. S F O . F A D . N Y E . . .
A R P . F U D G E . A M P E D
P E A C E T I M E . M A A . .
E X P O . S E A L S . U P O N
. E L I . T I M E P I E C E .
R E R A N . E L E N A . R T E
E X P . S A D . S I M . . . .
D O L A P S . S E E N O T E .
S T A G . D O W N S T A I R S
E I N E . O V I D . E N E M Y
A C E S . I A M S . R A D A R
```

6

```
J E A N . C H I L I . W H E Y
A X L E . T O N A L . H A L E
V A S T . A B B I E . O W N S
A M O N G . B A N D B . A I M
. . E R R E D . U R S I N E .
B O R G I A S . E D I T I O N
O N H A N D . A M I G A . . .
B O O T . I N D I A . N A D A
. . I N C A S . B O D I E S .
L A T V I A N . A L L U R E S
A S W E L L . S L E E P . . .
S P A . E L V E S . O G D E N
T I N A . E A T A T . U R G E
E R G O . F L I C K . Y O G A
D E S K . T E N E T . S P O T
```
(Circled letters in puzzle 6 spell: T E N D E G U R A L E E F)

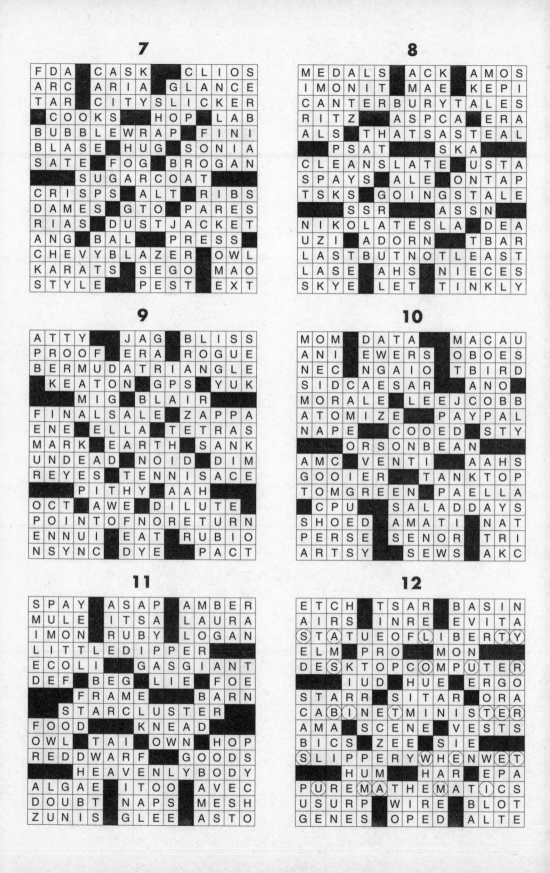

7

F	D	A		C	A	S	K		C	L	I	O	S
A	R	C		A	R	I	A		G	L	A	N	C	E
T	A	R		C	I	T	Y	S	L	I	C	K	E	R
	C	O	O	K	S			H	O	P		L	A	B
B	U	B	B	L	E	W	R	A	P		F	I	N	I
B	L	A	S	E		H	U	G		S	O	N	I	A
S	A	T	E		F	O	G		B	R	O	G	A	N
			S	U	G	A	R	C	O	A	T			
C	R	I	S	P	S		A	L	T		R	I	B	S
D	A	M	E	S		G	T	O		P	A	R	E	S
R	I	A	S		D	U	S	T	J	A	C	K	E	T
A	N	G		B	A	L		P	R	E	S	S		
C	H	E	V	Y	B	L	A	Z	E	R		O	W	L
K	A	R	A	T	S		S	E	G	O		M	A	O
S	T	Y	L	E		P	E	S	T		E	X	T	

8

M	E	D	A	L	S		A	C	K		A	M	O	S
I	M	O	N	I	T		M	A	E		K	E	P	I
C	A	N	T	E	R	B	U	R	Y	T	A	L	E	S
R	I	T	Z		A	S	P	C	A		E	R	A	
A	L	S		T	H	A	T	S	A	S	T	E	A	L
	P	S	A	T			S	K	A					
C	L	E	A	N	S	L	A	T	E		U	S	T	A
S	P	A	Y	S		A	L	E		O	N	T	A	P
T	S	K	S		G	O	I	N	G	S	T	A	L	E
	S	S	R			A	S	S	N					
N	I	K	O	L	A	T	E	S	L	A		D	E	A
U	Z	I		A	D	O	R	N		T	B	A	R	
L	A	S	T	B	U	T	N	O	T	L	E	A	S	T
L	A	S	E		A	H	S		N	I	E	C	E	S
S	K	Y	E		L	E	T		T	I	N	K	L	Y

9

A	T	T	Y		J	A	G		B	L	I	S	S
P	R	O	O	F		E	R	A		R	O	G	U	E
B	E	R	M	U	D	A	T	R	I	A	N	G	L	E
	K	E	A	T	O	N		G	P	S		Y	U	K
		M	I	G		B	L	A	I	R				
F	I	N	A	L	S	A	L	E		Z	A	P	P	A
E	N	E		E	L	L	A		T	E	T	R	A	S
M	A	R	K		E	A	R	T	H		S	A	N	K
U	N	D	E	A	D		N	O	I	D		D	I	M
R	E	Y	E	S		T	E	N	N	I	S	A	C	E
		P	I	T	H	Y		A	A	H				
O	C	T		A	W	E		D	I	L	U	T	E	
P	O	I	N	T	O	F	N	O	R	E	T	U	R	N
E	N	N	U	I		E	A	T		R	U	B	I	O
N	S	Y	N	C		D	Y	E		P	A	C	T	

10

M	O	M		D	A	T	A		M	A	C	A	U
A	N	I		E	W	E	R	S		O	B	O	E	S
N	E	C		N	G	A	I	O		T	B	I	R	D
S	I	D	C	A	E	S	A	R		A	N	O		
M	O	R	A	L	E		L	E	E	J	C	O	B	B
A	T	O	M	I	Z	E		P	A	Y	P	A	L	
N	A	P	E		C	O	O	E	D		S	T	Y	
			O	R	S	O	N	B	E	A	N			
A	M	C		V	E	N	T	I		A	A	H	S	
G	O	O	I	E	R		T	A	N	K	T	O	P	
T	O	M	G	R	E	E	N		P	A	E	L	L	A
	C	P	U		S	A	L	A	D	D	A	Y	S	
S	H	O	E	D		A	M	A	T	I		N	A	T
P	E	R	S	E		S	E	N	O	R		T	R	I
A	R	T	S	Y		S	E	W	S		A	K	C	

11

S	P	A	Y		A	S	A	P		A	M	B	E	R
M	U	L	E		I	T	S	A		L	A	U	R	A
I	M	O	N		R	U	B	Y		L	O	G	A	N
L	I	T	T	L	E	D	I	P	P	E	R			
E	C	O	L	I		G	A	S	G	I	A	N	T	
D	E	F		B	E	G		L	I	E		F	O	E
		F	R	A	M	E			B	A	R	N		
	S	T	A	R	C	L	U	S	T	E	R			
F	O	O	D		K	N	E	A	D					
O	W	L		T	A	I		O	W	N		H	O	P
R	E	D	D	W	A	R	F		G	O	O	D	S	
	H	E	A	V	E	N	L	Y	B	O	D	Y		
A	L	G	A	E		I	T	O	O		A	V	E	C
D	O	U	B	T		N	A	P	S		M	E	S	H
Z	U	N	I	S		G	L	E	E		A	S	T	O

12

E	T	C	H		T	S	A	R		B	A	S	I	N
A	I	R	S		I	N	R	E		E	V	I	T	A
(S)	T	A	T	U	E	O	F	L	I	B	E	R	T	(Y)
E	L	M		P	R	O			M	O	N			
D	E	S	K	T	O	P	C	O	M	P	U	T	E	R
	I	U	D		H	U	E		E	R	G	O		
S	T	A	R	R		S	I	T	A	R		O	R	A
C	A	B	I	N	E	T	M	I	N	I	S	T	E	R
A	M	A		S	C	E	N	E		V	E	S	T	S
B	I	C	S		Z	E	E		S	I	E			
S	L	I	P	P	E	R	Y	W	H	E	N	W	E	T
	H	U	M		H	A	R		E	P	A			
P	U	R	E	M	A	T	H	E	M	A	T	I	C	S
U	S	U	R	P		W	I	R	E		B	L	O	T
G	E	N	E	S		O	P	E	D		A	L	T	E

13

```
X R A Y S   C A W   L E T U P S
M I X E R   A M O   U T O P I A
A L L S I K N O W   C H O S E N
S E E M   N O N   T K O S
    A L O N G W A Y S O F F
S T R A I T   A N Y   O L A F
T R U M P   A R G O   N A I L
E O N   S T A K E O U T   G L O
M I S O   O A R S   O B O E S
S K I D   P H O   T R E N D S
  A N D T H E N I S A Y S
    S E E D   H O G   T R E E
H A V A N A   H O W S A B O U T
I M P R O V   A P E   G U A R D
M I S E R Y   L E D   T Y R O S
```

14

```
S W A P   C R O C   D R A M A
H E I R   O A T H   E U L E R
A L D O   N I T E   A D E L E
G L E N N C L O S E L Y
      T E E   T A M   E A P
    H O W A R D S T E R N L Y
P S A   L E O   I N T E R
E A R N S   G N U   N A I V E
S T R I P   O N O   T E X
T A Y L O R S W I F T L Y
O N S   R I P   F A A
    J A M E S B L U N T L Y
U R G E D   C H A I   D R E I
S A U D I   K I L N   R E A P
C Y N I C   S A K E   Y E N S
```

15

```
E G O S   V A P O R   I R I S
B E R T   I R A T E   N A T L
B E E R B A T T E R   E C H O
S K O A L   E R A S   H A T
    P U M P K I N C O A C H
S K I   R O E   R H E A S
O I L S   N A S A   A F L
B A L L P A R K F I G U R E S
  B A E   S A L T   N A P A
A L E V E   A C T   Y A P
W A T E R P I T C H E R
N T H   S U M O   R E A M S
I T E M   C E I L I N G F A N
N E R O   K A L E L   A R I A
G R E W   S N E A K   L O N G
```

16

```
X F L   G R A T E   S T A I D
E R A   R E L A Y   C O S M O
N O S E R V I C E   R A Y O N
O D E A   O B I   P E S O
N O R S E L I T E R A T U R E
    T U T   G E M   W A X
E M B E R   S A G E   M I N I
N E U R O S C I E N T I S T S
D A R N   C U R D   I M H O T
O R S   J A B   V E E
N A T I O N A L P A S T I M E
  O N U S   Y I P   I C O N
J A P E S   P I N O C C H I O
E X E R T   I N T R O   A R K
T E N T S   A G A S P   T A I
```

17

```
W I S H   L A M B   S W A M I
A K I O   A L O E   I O N I C
S E C L U S I O N   G E N R E
P A K I S T A N Z A N I A
      D E N       P H S
N I C A R A G U A T E M A L A
O K A Y   M O N K   R E B A R
E N C   G E N T I L E   N Y E
L O T S A   E I R E   D E E N
S W I T Z E R L A N D O R R A
      O E D       T A M
    U N I T E D N A T I O N S
T A K E N   B E A N A N G E L
A V E R T   A C I D   O L I O
B A S S O   Y O L O   S E N T
```

18

```
W D S   C D R O M   A P B I O
I R A   A W A R E   C L U C K
L U L U L E M O N   H A D E S
S N A R L E R   L O N G S
O K R A   B O O B O O B E A R
N S Y N C   D U A L   T W O
    I O S   R B I   R E S T
  P U P U P L A T T E R
P R I M   R E A   A I L
I O N   E T D S   P A L E S
G O O G O O E Y E S   P I T A
  S C A R F   A M U S E R S
E T H I C   V U V U Z E L A S
D E L T A   O T E R I   O D E
D R E S S   N E R F S   W E D
```

19

```
S E E S   E T T E     L A S S
T I L T   R E A R S   A R I A
A R E A   A S S A I   R A T S
R E A L I S T     S T I L E S
      E T E S   A S E A
A L T A I R   A L I S T E R
S A R I S   R I T E S   L A T
S T I R   S E L E S   R I T A
T E T   S T E E R   E A T E R
  R E T A I L S   A T R E S T
    E L L S   E S A I
I S R A E L   S A L T I E R
R I I S   E T A T S   I R A E
E L L E   R E L E E   E A S E
S T E R     L E S T   S S T S
```

20

```
H T M L   C H E F   P S A L M
O W E S   I O T A   E E R I E
W O R D S A L A D   G A P E D
T A M   W O E   I R A T E
O M A H A   E N O S     G M T
  N O T H I N G B U R G E R
    T H I R D   S E I N E
S W I M   P A N S Y   D O S E
P O S I T   O P E N S
C O U C H P O T A T O E S
A L P   R O L E   B A N G S
  P R I E D   G E E   I O U
S E O U L   H U M B L E P I E
E A S E L   A R A B   M E N D
T R E S S   T I N S   U R G E
```

21

```
I R A Q   T R I G   C B G B S
M E N T   R O S A   H E L O T
B O D Y G U A R D   I B I Z A
U R I   A I D   G A M E B O Y
E G E S T S   N E V E
    C O M P U T E R P O R T
S A M E   S E Z   C A R V E S
P R A N K   Z Z Z   S I E N A
A G R E E S   L I I   O N E R
M O V I E T H E A T E R
    P E A S   S A Y I D O
I C E L A N D   C O S   M E X
B O R A T   F R O N T P A G E
M I T Z I   U N U M   A G U Y
S L E E T   N A P E   H O M E
```

22

```
J A G S   P E P E   B R O M O
A C U P   E X I T   R E N E W
I N S I S T E N T   A H E M S
L E T T H E M E A T C A K E
      E A R P   R E S
  O F F W I T H H E R H E A D
U H A U L   Y U K S   B E E
C A R L   D O P E S   H E R B
L I S   L O A N   S A R I S
A R I E A N T O I N E T T E
    S T U   S O R T
  C A P I T A L O F F E N S E
M O U R N   S A L E S R O O M
C U R I O   T I D E   A D A M
S P A T S   A C E S   S E R A
```

23

```
B L O C K E D   N A H   O H M
R O M A N C E   A T A   N O R
A N N I E O A K L E Y   C O B
S E I N E   R I D O F   E P I
      E L S   N I N E B A L L
U N C   S I P     V I R A L
G R O W   F R A T   E G O
H A M I L T O N B E R M U D A
  P E A   S T A T   E N I D
G R A S P     R A H   D E O
R E N T R O L L   L E I
I V Y   O B O E S   I D A H O
T E M   B E S T M U S I C A L
T R A   E Y E   E S T O N I A
Y E N   S S R   W E S T E R N
```

24

```
G P A   M A G O O   S C O W S
O L D   C L O T H   I O N I A
B A D   E L L E F A N N I N G
I N L A W   R U N   C O D E
G E E Y A T H I N K   E N C
      E N Y A   H A R S H
A N T S   P R O M   I N O I L
S E E   B E E B A L M   U M A
K I T T Y   S I L O   A P E X
  L E A S E     I N S T
    Y A K   T E A K E T T L E S
N O T E   T L C   A N G L E
C U E T H E M U S I C   B I C
A N T E S   S T A R K   T O T
A G E N T   T E X A S   Q T S
```

25

T	A	C	T	■	O	C	A	L	A	■	R	A	M	P
E	C	H	O	■	M	O	R	E	L	■	O	D	I	E
S	N	E	A	K	A	P	E	E	K	■	L	E	A	D
H	E	A	D	O	N	■	T	R	A	V	O	L	T	A
■	■	P	S	A	■	S	E	A	L	A	D	E	A	L
O	D	D	■	L	O	P	■	T	I	N	E	■	■	■
G	R	A	B	A	C	A	B	■	■	E	X	U	L	T
L	E	T	O	■	T	R	A	D	E	■	E	S	A	U
E	W	E	R	S	■	■	G	O	T	A	S	H	O	T
■	■	■	D	A	S	H	■	Z	A	P	■	I	S	U
B	A	K	E	A	C	A	K	E	■	N	H	S	■	■
W	E	L	L	B	O	R	N	■	K	E	A	T	O	N
A	R	I	L	■	W	R	O	T	E	A	N	O	T	E
N	O	N	O	■	L	I	T	E	R	■	G	R	O	W
A	S	K	S	■	S	S	T	A	R	■	S	Y	S	T

26

P	E	A	R	■	E	B	O	N	Y	■	M	O	R	A	L
A	R	I	A	■	B	E	N	E	S	■	A	M	A	Z	E
C	A	M	I	N	O	R	E	A	L	■	Y	E	N	T	A
■	■	■	S	O	L	E	S	■	■	■	G	O	E	S	■
■	P	R	I	V	A	T	E	E	N	T	R	A	N	C	E
A	L	A	N	■	■	C	L	O	N	E	S	■	■	■	■
R	E	S	E	N	D	S	■	L	O	O	M	■	S	P	A
C	A	P	T	A	I	N	F	A	N	T	A	S	T	I	C
S	T	Y	■	G	A	U	L	■	S	E	X	T	A	N	T
■	■	■	F	A	R	C	E	S	■	■	A	N	T	S	■
Q	W	E	R	T	Y	K	E	Y	B	O	A	R	D	S	■
A	H	M	E	■	■	■	D	E	A	N	S	■	■	■	■
T	O	A	S	T	■	I	N	N	E	R	C	H	I	L	D
A	L	I	C	E	■	S	C	E	N	E	■	I	D	E	A
R	E	L	A	X	■	T	O	Y	E	D	■	P	O	N	Y

27

R	A	F	T	■	C	A	P	S	I	D	■	P	E	P
A	R	I	A	■	O	R	A	C	L	E	■	O	N	O
W	A	R	N	I	N	G	S	H	O	T	■	O	R	S
B	L	E	N	D	S	■	■	U	S	E	D	P	O	T
A	S	H	E	S	■	I	M	S	E	R	I	O	U	S
R	E	A	D	■	A	M	I	S	■	■	T	U	T	U
S	A	T	■	L	I	A	R	■	I	N	S	T	E	P
■	■	N	O	R	M	A	L	D	A	Y	■	■	■	■
D	E	V	I	L	S	■	C	O	I	N	■	B	A	S
A	L	E	C	■	■	S	L	O	G	■	K	A	L	E
B	A	N	K	R	A	T	E	S	■	B	I	B	L	E
E	P	I	S	O	D	E	■	■	L	A	D	Y	D	I
A	S	S	■	A	F	R	I	C	A	N	L	I	O	N
R	E	O	■	S	E	N	T	U	P	■	I	S	N	T
S	S	N	■	T	E	S	T	E	D	■	T	H	E	O

28

S	W	I	S	S	■	I	K	E	■	C	A	S	I	N	O
P	O	R	C	H	■	S	O	X	■	E	S	C	R	O	W
O	T	E	R	I	■	B	R	O	■	O	P	I	A	T	E
C	A	N	O	P	E	N	E	R	■	■	E	S	S	E	S
K	N	E	L	L	S	■	A	C	O	R	N	S	■	■	■
■	■	L	O	P	■	N	I	K	E	■	O	N	T	O	■
A	G	E	■	A	N	T	■	S	A	P	■	R	A	I	N
P	A	R	T	D	■	A	R	M	Y	■	N	S	Y	N	C
S	L	A	W	■	T	R	A	■	S	R	O	■	S	T	E
E	L	S	E	■	S	P	C	A	■	A	A	A	■	■	■
■	■	E	R	A	S	E	D	■	C	H	R	I	S	T	■
C	R	A	Z	E	■	■	C	O	R	K	S	C	R	E	W
L	O	V	E	T	O	■	A	N	O	■	A	T	A	R	I
E	M	E	R	I	L	■	R	I	O	■	R	A	N	I	N
F	E	S	S	E	D	■	S	S	T	■	K	N	I	F	E

29

H	I	T	O	N	■	A	L	E	■	S	I	L	T
A	D	O	R	E	■	A	L	E	C	■	O	B	I	E
T	O	N	G	U	E	L	A	S	H	■	C	E	L	T
P	I	G	■	T	A	D	■	S	O	C	K	E	Y	E
I	D	A	■	R	E	M	O	■	L	E	N	■	■	■
N	O	N	P	C	■	N	A	N	■	E	T	H	E	R
■	■	A	O	R	T	A	■	D	A	S	A	N	I
I	M	I	N	A	W	E	■	B	O	R	E	D	O	M
P	A	N	T	R	Y	■	T	R	O	U	T	■	■	■
O	T	R	O	S	■	P	O	E	■	P	S	Y	C	H
■	■	E	M	E	■	A	I	W	A	■	E	O	E
S	A	T	I	N	O	N	■	S	H	H	■	M	R	I
P	L	U	M	■	H	A	S	K	I	T	T	E	N	S
O	G	R	E	■	O	M	N	I	■	T	E	N	E	T
T	A	N	S	■	K	A	L	■	P	A	I	R	S

30

C	B	S	■	J	O	N	I	■	E	N	T	I	R	E
A	L	E	■	B	A	R	A	K	■	L	O	O	N	E	Y
G	O	L	D	E	N	A	G	E	■	S	C	Y	T	H	E
I	N	F	I	D	E	L	S	■	K	I	A	■	H	E	D
E	D	I	T	H	■	B	A	N	N	E	R	Y	E	A	R
R	E	E	S	E	S	■	T	E	A	■	B	O	W	T	O
■	■	■	A	U	G	■	A	V	G	■	G	A	S	P
■	R	E	D	L	E	T	T	E	R	D	A	Y	■	■	■
M	A	U	I	■	K	I	R	■	S	A	O	■	■	■
U	M	B	R	A	■	S	I	B	■	D	O	G	M	A	S
F	I	N	E	S	T	H	O	U	R	■	D	R	A	K	E
F	R	O	■	C	I	A	■	M	A	I	L	I	T	I	N
L	I	S	P	E	D	■	P	R	I	M	E	T	I	M	E
E	T	E	R	N	E	■	C	A	S	A	S	■	N	B	C
R	E	S	E	T	S	■	S	P	E	X	■	G	O	A

31

```
INCA FINIS  BUCK
LEAN EVITA  ASIA
LIPIZZANER  SETH
SLOMO NEMO  EDEN
   ANN    NUT
 MILKOFMAGNESIA
MASS SLID  INERT
URL REARLIT  RAM
SLATE MEAN  GUTS
HAMMEREDITHOME
   ODE    OUR
BLAB GOSH  LEAPT
AUDI GREYMATTER
RAIL AANDE  EASE
DUNE ELDER  XBOX
```

32

```
BOZO DEAN   JILT
ARES ELMO  WADES
TESLACOIL  EBOOK
HOTOIL  DELL
ESS  DAB  SILENTI
  HARRISONFORD
CII  EEC  NOFOOL
MANGY WEE  WISPY
ONAHOP UPI  GEE
LINCOLNPENNY
TOESHOE  EDU  CPA
  OPEC  IDCHIP
SETTO  DODGEBALL
ALOES  BONO  ESAU
TIRE  ETAS  REFS
```

33

```
COBS AGAVE  FACE
LION BALER  ELAL
ALBA EIDER  LEGO
UMBRELLAPOLICY
DELLA   LOX
ENE RUM  JFK  FOE
 HAPPYHOLIDAYS
AMEN READY  RILE
STAYFORDINNER
PAD LAS  ENS  ECO
  OUR    FINAL
 BABEINTHEWOODS
DOZE OOHED  TUDE
UZIS UTURN  AGIN
OOZE SIDEA  SHES
```

34

```
ADEPT ALSO  UPON
HAVEI DAUB  VILE
ALIEN ODDS  UNDO
BILLYCRYSTAL
   TOE  AMATOL
JOLTIN SPCA  IRE
ALARM RAULJULIA
MESO PENNE  VEES
JOHNCANDY  BERNE
ALE  ARTY  BEASTS
RESORT  FOR
  BOYMEETSGIRL
HALE IONA  ERNIE
ALAS NAYS  RIFFS
JIBE GNAT  KNOTS
```

35

```
WORM LESS  GRETA
AREA AMTS  LUXOR
LIPS BEESTUDENT
LOOKHERE  ATOM
ELS ALINES  LPGA
TEEBILL  DEEFLAT
  IRE WARM  APE
 SONG DIM  PURE
DEF EDEN  JRS
EXFILES  CUEBERT
STIR CIGARS  NEE
 CIAO EPISODES
GEESTRINGS  PULL
EGRET ROUT  ARIA
MOSSY SANS  LENS
```

36

```
HOPI GALLS  SLOG
ALAN ABOUT  WAVE
JIGS LEONE  IMAN
IVE ROTTENAPPLE
SETTERS  CUE
 URGE THINSKIN
PARIS SHALT  ETE
LYNX DUETS  BLEW
OLE GRIME  BALMS
PARFAITS  BONY
 LIL  VINEGAR
URBANLEGEND  RTE
VOOM BLING  DEAL
EASE ISSUE  JERI
ARCS TETES  SNIT
```

37

```
R I S K ■ S A R O N G ■ ■ ■ D I M
I N S I S T S U P O N ■ C O D A
M A N C H E S T E R U N I T E D
■ ■ K I W I ■ ■ ■ ■ O N E A M
M I S S I S S I P P I D E L T A
A R A B S ■ I M L A T E ■ L E X
H O K U M ■ P E R I S H ■ ■
I C E T ■ C A R A T S ■ I D O L
■ ■ T A L K E D ■ A G I N G
A M P ■ C U E S T A ■ S H R U B
S O U T H B Y S O U T H W E S T
I N T W O ■ ■ ■ D E B I ■
A I R P O R T T E R M I N A L S
N C I S ■ P R I D E A N D J O Y
S A D ■ M A L A Y S ■ S A W S
```

38

```
■ B L A S T S ■ E R E C T ■
■ A L A S K A N ■ G E T O U T
T H E P H I L O S O P H E R S
B O S S ■ R E B A T E ■ D N A
A T T E S T ■ W I N ■ ■
■ ■ A S P S ■ S T A L L S
A S L A N ■ E T A T ■ K E E N
G H I J K ■ R O W ■ L I N G O
A U R A ■ L E N O ■ E N D O W
S T E R E O ■ E L L A ■ ■
■ ■ N Y E ■ A P P L E T
A B A ■ D A R W I N ■ R I F E
D A N I E L R A D C L I F F E
A S N E A T ■ S N E E Z E S
■ H A R R Y ■ P O T T E R ■
```

39

```
S H A H ■ C R O O N ■ C P A S
P A C A ■ H I P P O ■ A R N O
E T A L ■ A F T E R ■ R E A L
W H I F F O F S C A N D A L
■ ■ L E S S ■ ■ O I L ■
■ S U I T ■ A D S L O G A N
F A N F A V O R I T E ■ E M O
O L D E ■ A U T R Y ■ R B I S
U S E ■ S T R I K E F O R C E
L A R G E S S E ■ E S A I ■
■ W A G ■ ■ O K I E ■
■ G O D O W N S W I N G I N G
W O R F ■ E A T I N ■ O K A Y
B I L L ■ S P A N K ■ L E A R
A N D Y ■ T A N G Y ■ D A N E
```

40

```
J A P A N ■ S O L O ■ R A N D
I R A T E ■ T W I N ■ A L O E
L A S E R G U I D E D B O M B
T B S ■ F O R E ■ O R A T E S
■ ■ A G E D ■ S N I T ■
F O S B U R Y F L O P ■ S I P
A S T I N ■ R O N ■ L A N A
I C E D ■ B R I B E ■ A J A R
L A N E ■ R O E ■ G I A N T
S R O ■ R O A S T T U R K E Y
■ ■ H E A D ■ V A T S ■
S H I E L D ■ R I C H ■ H A S
H O L L Y W O O D O R B U S T
E L S E ■ A R L O ■ I O N I A
D E A N ■ Y E L L ■ E D G A R
```

41

```
F O I L ■ V A N S ■ A S P C A
U P D O ■ E L A L ■ R E L A X
J A Y G A T S B Y ■ S A U T E
I L L ■ R O O S ■ S E E M S
■ ■ H O E ■ M A N E T ■
■ Y O U A R E N O T A L O N E
T O N E R ■ N A D A L ■ M I R
O K A Y ■ S T A I N ■ M A X I
M E L ■ E P I C S ■ P U T O N
E L L E M A C P H E R S O N
■ F L U M E ■ ■ N O S ■
■ T O I L S ■ S E A M ■ T N T
G O U D A ■ W H Y B O T H E R
E G R E T ■ E A R L ■ A R I A
M A S S E ■ T H E E ■ J U L Y
```

42

```
A B E ■ T O U C H ■ P S S T
M A C S ■ I O N I A ■ U C L A
A L O H A S H I R T ■ P R O S
S I C E M ■ T R E E ■ E V E
S H A L O M M E I R T O W E R
E A R ■ R I O ■ S H R I N E
S I S I ■ N O P E ■ A C T E D
■ ■ P A X R O M A N A ■ ■
S O S A D ■ S P I T ■ S A C K
A R T S E T ■ T I C ■ S H E
M I R S P A C E S T A T I O N
P G A ■ T I R E ■ R E S I N
R A P T ■ W O R L D P E A C E
A M I S ■ A N I T A ■ D I E D
S I N K ■ N E E D Y ■ D R Y
```

43

```
P A S S ■ J D A T E ■ A T I T
A R T I ■ P I N O N ■ F I N I
P E A C H E S A N D C R E A M
A N N ■ A G A ■ I O U ■ S W E
Y A C H T ■ S A C R E D C O W
A S H E ■ A T V ■ ■ N O R A ■
■ ■ R O M E O ■ H O A R D S ■
■ P O W E R C O U P L E ■ ■ ■
P E R I L S ■ A P N E A ■ ■ ■
E L O N ■ ■ D U G ■ B A N D ■
A C T E D C O O L ■ E S S I E
T H E ■ O A F ■ E O S ■ P E C
B A C K G R O U N D C H E C K
O P T O ■ P L A C E ■ I C E E
G O S S ■ I D L E S ■ P T S D
```

44

```
■ S T R A W ■ ■ C D S ■ H A M
S P E E D O ■ D R E W ■ I D O
A I R F O R C E O N E ■ T E X
I N N S ■ S U M O ■ E C O L I
L E S ■ S T R I K E T H R E E
■ ■ ■ R A S ■ ■ L I A M ■ ■ ■
L A T E X ■ G I M M E F I V E
A L I T ■ M O V E S ■ I S E E
G A M E S E V E N ■ A N S E L
■ E L A N ■ ■ ■ U G G ■ ■ ■ ■
O N C L O U D N I N E ■ R A M
B E A S T ■ I O N S ■ J U D O
E A R ■ O D D S A N D E N D S
Y T D ■ M I N E ■ A U D I T S
S O S ■ E N T ■ G E I C O ■ ■
```

45

```
C H A L L A H ■ ■ L E F T S ■
S A T I A T E ■ B E T R U E ■
I N V E S T S ■ T R I C O R N
■ S T A I R C A S E W I T ■ ■
■ I T S ■ T O B Y ■ T N N ■ ■
■ E C O ■ M A C Y ■ F E E ■ ■
A L E ■ B A N K ■ S O R D I D
E S C A L A T O R C L A U S E
R E U N E S ■ P O R K ■ P E W
■ B T W ■ R E M Y ■ D O E ■ ■
■ G E E ■ D O R A ■ M A N ■ ■
O N T H E U P A N D U P ■ ■ ■
S A R A L E E ■ C O S P L A Y
S T A L L S ■ ■ E V I L E Y E
A S Y L A ■ ■ ■ S E C E D E S
```

46

```
■ W A S A B I ■ E N D A S H ■
F O R E M A N ■ V A U N T E D
R O N Z O N I ■ E V E N P A R
O H O ■ ■ S T O L E ■ A R I ■
D O L E D ■ T O K ■ C A U S E
O O D L E S O F N O O D L E S
■ ■ ■ F L O W ■ I N N S ■ ■ ■
P E A ■ A N I S E E D ■ S H E
L A I T Y ■ N O V ■ O S H E A
A G R A ■ A I D E D ■ L E N S
N E T C O S T ■ L E S A B R E
E R R O R S ■ ■ P O B O Y S ■
■ ■ A B B Y C A D A B B Y ■ ■
G A V E ■ R A R E R ■ I G G Y
A X E L ■ I S L E T ■ N A P E
Y E L L ■ A T O M S ■ G N A T
```

47

```
S P E W ■ A D A P T S ■ R A M
A L T I ■ E S C A R P ■ E N O
M E A N T T H E W O R L D T O
S A L D A N A ■ L E A S E D ■
■ ■ S M A R T A L E C K ■ ■ ■
A R G O ■ P A D ■ ■ T E R A ■
B A R R E D ■ N A U T I L U S
A D A ■ L U C K Y M E ■ T S K
F I N A L O U T ■ P E L O S I
T O D D ■ J O S ■ ■ A N O N ■
■ ■ J O B H O P P I N G ■ ■ ■
B A U B L E ■ E N C A S E S ■
S P R E A D T H E G O S P E L
I S O ■ I D O I D O ■ S A G A
X E R ■ R A W E S T ■ E T S Y
```

48

```
T R E K ■ W A N N A ■ P E P S
Y A L E ■ I N B E D ■ E L I E
P I K E P L A C E M A R K E T
O N S P E C ■ ■ E L M E R S ■
■ ■ ■ L A O S ■ B N A I ■ ■ ■
M A C E S ■ T A I ■ S T P A T
A S O F ■ P A N D A ■ M U L E
G I F T ■ L I T E R ■ E G G S
O A F ■ M A R I N E R ■ E A T
O N E T O N ■ ■ N A N T E S ■
■ ■ E U L E R ■ S A T E S ■ ■
W A S T E ■ I S T ■ R O O T S
H U H ■ S P A T U L A ■ U R N
I D O ■ T I T A N I C ■ N I A
Z I P ■ S E A T T L E ■ D O G
```

49

```
C A B   M A M M A   A T H O S
L S U   A D I O S   B R U N T
O H M Y S T A R S   C A N O E
R O P E S   A A A   W K R P
O R E S   H O L Y T O L E D O
X E R   P E P   S E L   R E N
    E E R I E   D E E R E
  I L L B E D A R N E D
I S T O O   S P E A R
N E A   S I N   S A G   L O O
W E L L I N E V E R   B E E B
A T I E   K I R   A R G U E
R O A M S   G O O D G R A V Y
D I N O S   H O W I E   T R E
S T O N E   S M E A R   O E D
```

50

```
B A N D B   M S G   F J O R D
A G O R A   A I R   L E N T O
R E T A G   I R E   O T T E R
B R I G H T L I G H T S
S S N   D O E   O S A K A
  C A N D I D C A M E R A
M Y B A D   O V U M   V I N
A A R P   H A N D S   V I E D
S K A   T O N I   P A N S Y
C O V E R T A C T I O N
  V E N U E   A S K   U N A
  F I L M D I R E C T O R
A U T O S   A I L   M O T E T
P S A L M   Z O O   O P E N S
T E N D S   E R R   N E R D Y
```

51

```
S P A T   S P E N T   Q T I P
O R C A   S A R A H   U R S A
C O M M O N T I M E   I O T A
K N E E L   E N E   A C T O R
S E S S I O N   D U N K
  V E T E R A N S D A Y
F O D D E R   P O E   A E R O
A M I E S   P I P   S N E A K
N A R C   O R C   T O D D L E
G R E A T V I S I O N
  T R A M   C E N T R A L
P U S H Y   E C O   E R O D E
O P E L   E V E N S T E V E N
O T T O   S A D I E   M E L T
L O I N   E L E C T   E R E S
```

52

```
H I P S   P E C S   T W I S T
A C A I   A X L E   V E S P A
R E N T A L C A R   T I E U P
M U S H R O O M B U R G E R
S P Y   S O N   R A H
  W O K   C O S Y   E A T
  S P I N A C H L A S A G N A
A I R S   L E I   L A T E
B L A C K B E A N C H I L I
S T Y   L O F T   R U T
  L U I   A I M   A S H
  M E A T L E S S M O N D A Y
W A L T Z   B I K E R O U T E
I R A T E   B R E A   P L A N
G E N E S   S E W N   E T N A
```

53

```
I N S E A M   S T A B   P H D
T A T A M I   O H H I   H O E
A T A R I S   P A S S P O R T
L E N   S I S I   T E N S E
  D U E T O   P R A Y E R
G U I N N E S S B O O K
O F N O T E   I R I S   B T U
B O G S   N I X O N   B I A S
I S O   M U S E   T O O T L E
  C A S H R E G I S T E R
P A G O D A   P U L S E
I L I A D   P I S A   R T E
P A S T A B A R   R E P E A L
E M T   S A C K   D A U N T S
S O S   H A T S   S U N D A E
```

54

```
S W E P T   W E N D Y S   S A D
W A L L E   I D I O T S   E M O
U R B A N L E G E N D S   C P U
M E A N   A L E C   B U L B
  K I N D R E D S P I R I T
  B E T T E   Y O U B E T
H A L O S   S E A L U P   L U V
A S I N   T H E G A P   B I D E
Y E W   T O U L O N   T E N E T
  R H E S U S   S U L K S
Q U I C K T H I N K I N G
U N T O   T I N S   R A M P
I N N   G O O G L E I M A G E S
L E E   I N F U L L   O D O R S
T R Y   S T A Y A T   B E G E T
```

55

```
V A T S   O Z A R K   T G I F
C L U E   R O S I N   U R G E
H O S E   G O T T O   G A L E
I N C   B Y M O U T H   N O D
P E A B O   I R A   M S D O S
    L L B   N I L   O A F
  F O O   F O A L S   N O W
S W O O P I N   Y E W T R E E
K I S M E T     C H A K R A
A W A I T   P A C   I M S E T
    N A V A L H E R O
A G O G   E M B E R   N O G O
B L O T   S P A R E   I D E A
B O Z O   P A N I C   C O R K
A M E N   A S Y E T   A R M Y
```

56

```
A C I D   E N T E R   N E S S
S U M O   G O U G E   A L O T
S T U B B O R N A S A M U L E
N E P A L   D A D   L E D I N
      T A V I   T O L E D O
O N E T R I C K P O N Y
H A M L E T   A L O G   M A X
M I M E   T A R O T   B E R M
S L Y   S L I M   S I E S T A
      T H E L A W I S A A S S
A L P H A S   R E I N
R U R A L   C G I   A T T I C
O N O N E S H I G H H O R S E
S A N K   E I G H T   W I L L
E R G S   C A S T S   N O E L
```

57

```
R I C E   E F I L E   C R O P
O M A R   E A M E S   H I H O
T H I R T Y Q U E S T I O N S
C O N   R O S S   O N T O E
    O U R   C R O U P
F I F T E E N F O O T P O L E
A N A I S   O L M O S   L A B
I L L S   O B O E S   N I N O
N A S   A W O R D   N E C C O
T W E L V E D A Y S A W E E K
    H O R S Y   T N T
E C O L I   L O A N   H A I
T O O C L E V E R B Y H A L F
A L D A   M E T A L   B U F F
L A S T   S T O L E   O L A Y
```

58

```
P A P A   D U C K S   S P A N
E A R P   U R I A H   K A R O
W A I T S I N T H E W I N G S
  M E H   G L E E   D U H
  R E S E R V O I R D O G S
O U T T A K E   L A T H
R B I   F O R T   N O O S E S
E L M O   B B Q   H I R E
S E E P I N   S U E T   G I N
    A L E S   A B A S H E D
  M I L I T A R Y B R A T S
M A T   A C L U   S I S
B A C K D O O R S L I D E R S
A C H E   S N A R E   S E A L
S O Y A   T S L O T   O R G Y
```

59

```
S A N D   E G G E D   A M P M
C R E E D   V I O L A   B A R E
H A W A I I A N A I R   C F O S
I B M   D A N K   N O T I P S
S L O G A N   G R E E K V A S E
M E M O S   S O U N D S   D U D
  D E B T   D D E   L O P
  I N T E R M I S S I O N
S A O   T E E   I T R Y
I T D   O H W A I T   O A S I S
C A M O P A N T S   O N L I N E
A M I D S T   W A R M   N B A
R I T E   W I S E C R A C K E D
U N I T   A T T A R   N I E T O
S A T S   Y O U R E   D R A G
```

60

```
P S I   S O S P A D   L S D
O M G   P O M A D E   A P E
M A L A Y P E N I N S U L A
P R O F   S L E D   A R I D
  T O R T I L L A F L A T
      O W E   S E A
P A L E O       D A W E S
E G A D   H I C K   M A X X
A U K   D A S H E S   L P S
R A E   I L L I N I   L O W
    P E R F E C T G P A
  F L U K E   S H A W L
L E A D   M O O T   M A I L
A R C O   P A P A   P L E A
L A I R   T H A T   E L O N
A L D A   Y U L E   R A N D
```

61

```
H I P S . E N D O W . . S H A H
O M R I . V E R D I . . H O N E
M I S T R E S S E S . A T T A .
E N T . U S S . . E S P I E D .
L A U D S . . C I S T E R N S .
A W N U T S . O N T O . O N E .
B E T E . P R O D . R A N A T .
. . . L I F E L I N E S . . .
S P A S M . T E A R . S L I M .
A R T . H O A R . C R E E P O .
V I E W I N G S . . U T A H N .
A V I A T E . . J A B . D O O .
G Y N T . D I V E R S I O N S .
E T T E . G L A D E . T R E K .
D O O R . E L L I S . D E S I .
```

62

```
P A P E R . A P E S . . E T C H
L L A M A . R E P O . . T H O U
O P T I C . E R I C . . H E W N
W H I T E K N U C K L E D . .
S A O . D N A . . E U R O P A .
. . V I E . F I T S . . N O N .
G R E E N E Y E D . T R A I T .
N U N S . L O D E S . . E L S E
A B E T S . R E D H A N D E D .
S I R . A P E X . A M T . . .
H O G T I E . . A K A . P R O .
. . Y E L L O W B E L L I E D .
O R B S . T R A Y . G A T E D .
N E A T . E G G S . A T A L L .
S P R Y . D Y E S . M E S S Y .
```

63

```
A D D S . O M I T . . H O P E D
P R O W . F O R E . A N O D E .
A L G A . F R O S . G O R S E .
C A M P A I G N S I G N S . .
H U E . N C A A . N I E C E S .
E R A . G E N G H I S K H A N .
S A T I E . . E O N . N E R O .
. . D R I B . S K E E . . .
V O T E . M A A . R E S T S .
W R O N G A N S W E R . O A T .
S O N T A G . H I L O . A K A .
. S I L E N T P A R T N E R .
S P I K E . E R I N . H D T V .
O S L I N . L E N D . I S E E .
P A S T A . L E G S . S O N S .
```

64

```
A D D E R . D A B . A F T E R
D I A N A . E M U . D R O N E
H A N D Y . B I L . H O I T Y
O R D . G R U E L . E S T E E
C Y Y O U N G . M A R T Y R S
. . A N A . T O N E . . .
T R E K S . F O O D S T A M P
W A V E . H O T S Y . W I R E
O P E N H O U S E . D I D I N
. . . O P R Y . A I R . .
S T D E N I S . S C U L P T S
I H O P E . P O W E R . A A H
L O V E Y . E G O . N A M B Y
T R E E D . E R R . A M B L E
S A Y S O . D E N . L A Y E R
```

65

```
N E H I . W O K S . . D U B S
A D A M . R O O T S . A C L U
P U R P L E H A R T . L O I S
. D E E N . L E O . A N T I .
S T Y L E . P A W P R I N Z E
W E B . S K Y . . S A L . .
E T O N . F L A K . P A R I S
P R Y O R C O M M I T M E N T
T A S T E . N Y A D . A S E A
. . O E R . R A P . C R Y .
B A R R F I G H T . A B U T S
A C A I . F O E . T I R E .
M O P E . F A L L E N I D L E
B R I T . S P I E S . B O O N
I N D Y . E X I T . E G G O
```

66

```
F I S H . F L I P . H A R S H
O H H I . E O N S . A L I K E
C O O P . M U S I C N O T E S
A P T . F U N . U S N E W S .
L E T T E R G R A D E S . .
. O E R . E E L . L O F T S
S C H E M E . C A N . R I A .
C H E M I C A L S Y M B O L S
A I L . O U I . C E A S E S .
B A L E S . D N A . A L T . .
. . M O V I E R A T I N G S
M A R B L E . T I S . I R A .
B L O O D T Y P E S . A X E L
A B O D E . E A R L . H O E S
S A T Y R . S T Y E . A N K A
```

67

```
V O L G A ■ S W I F T ■ ■ T O E ■
I V I E D ■ L A D L E ■ H U T ■
B A L T I M O R E A N ■ I T E ■
E L Y S E E ■ H A M ■ U N I X
■ B U S H E L B A S K E T
D A L Y ■ M I R ■ E M U S ■
U N I ■ P E S O ■ I A M S O
C E N T E R ■ I S L A N D
T W E E T ■ M T N S ■ L E E
■ B E R G ■ Y A H ■ S L E D
S T A T I O N A G E N T
A R C H ■ H O N ■ L A R O S A
Y U K ■ F O R M A L T A L K S
A C E ■ A M M A N ■ A T E I T
H E R ■ T E A R Y ■ L A S S O
```

68

```
W E B ■ C Y A N ■ T I R A D E
I L L ■ H A R E ■ O N E M A N
R O D C A R E W ■ R A V I N G
E I G H T D A Y S A W E E K
■ A S S ■ O T H E R ■
E A R ■ B R A ■ S N A G
L A S T W E E K T O N I G H T
E T C ■ A T L ■ I S O ■ R O O
A M O N T H O F S U N D A Y S
F E T A ■ V A T ■ U M S
I N K E R ■ O F F
C A L E N D A R R E F O R M
T O N G U E ■ W A G E S W A R
M A T U R E ■ A T A D ■ I I I
S T E N O S ■ Y E N S ■ E D S
```

69

```
T H O R ■ R E A R M ■ N E O N
R E V E ■ E R G O T ■ E X P O
I L E S ■ A R G O N ■ V E T S
F I R E A L A R M ■ J E S S E
L U S T S ■ T E M P E R
E M T ■ S E A S A L T ■ O A F
■ A P E X ■ S T A ■ C U R E
K R Y P T O N ■ E N A C T E D
H O E S ■ D O E ■ E S S O
Z E D ■ P U B L I S H ■ F W D
■ M I S L E D ■ E M C E E
X E N O N ■ E M U L S I O N S
M A Y O ■ A G E N T ■ A U T O
E V E N ■ N A N N Y ■ T R O T
N E T S ■ A S T O R ■ A T N O
```

70

```
A S C O T ■ H U S H ■ F I B
G L O B E ■ P A L E O ■ I D O
R A D I A T O R C A P ■ L E O
A W E ■ U P P E R ■ M E A N
■ W I N D S O R C A S T L E
B O N G O ■ H I D
P A R L O R C A R ■ D E R B Y
O L D E ■ S H Y E R ■ G A L E
V I S A S ■ I N D O O R C A T
■ G R E ■ S W E E T
L I Q U O R C A B I N E T
A G U E ■ M O X I E ■ R A T
I L E ■ K I L L E R W H A L E
R O E ■ E N T E R ■ E M C E E
S O N ■ N E S S ■ T O K E N
```

71

```
M I C A ■ L O L A ■ A V E R
A T O N ■ I M A X ■ S P O R E
G E N T ■ P I G E O N C O O P
I M T O A S T ■ R O A D I E
■ I N D Y ■ I R A ■ L O C A
B A N Y A N ■ B A N ■ C O A L
C H U M P C H A N G E
C H E S T ■ E N G ■ S Q U I D
■ S U C K E R P U N C H
C C U P ■ C H E ■ E R O D E S
O R S O ■ O E R ■ D I V E
N E U R O N ■ B E T A R A Y
M A R K A N T O N Y ■ D O T E
E S P Y S ■ C R E E ■ I O T A
N E S S ■ M E G S ■ S S N S
```

72

```
I M D B ■ M A H I ■ S C A D S
M O U E ■ A S I F ■ A L L O W
A N C H O R A G E ■ G O P R O
C A K E D ■ P H A T ■ C H A R
■ B A E Z ■ W R E C K A G E
B A L D ■ I D A ■ E O S
O W I E ■ G U Y A N A ■ S A P
B O N D A G E ■ P I L L A G E
O L D ■ G U L P E D ■ A F R O
■ W A R ■ I D O ■ W E A N
C O V E R A G E ■ L A M S
R I O T ■ T E S T ■ N A P E S
A L I B I ■ S H R I N K A G E
M U L A N ■ S O O T ■ E C O N
S P A R K ■ O P T S ■ R E S T
```

73

H	A	D	J		W	I	L	L		S	P	R	A	Y	S
I	S	E	E		I	D	E	A		T	A	I	P	E	I
T	H	A	T	S	N	O	T	T	H	E	P	O	I	N	T
		S	O	D		I	O	T	A		E	T	A		
P	I	C	K	U	P	L	I	N	E		L	E	C	A	R
A	C	A	I		O	O	N	A		B	L	E	S	S	
L	E	I		A	W	E	D		P	I	U	S			
	S	N	A	K	E	S	O	N	A	P	L	A	N	E	
	E	R	R	S		O	R	A	L		A	X	E		
C	H	A	R	O		U	S	E	D		S	P	E	W	
L	O	G	O	N		I	N	E	E	D	S	P	A	C	E
E	R	E		O	K	R	A		R	I	A				
A	N	O	T	H	E	R	D	I	M	E	N	S	I	O	N
R	E	N	O	I	R		O	P	U	S		M	O	L	E
S	T	E	P	O	N		N	A	G	S		S	U	E	D

74

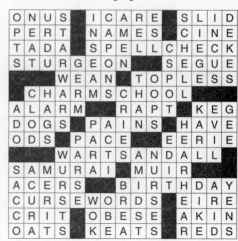

O	N	U	S		I	C	A	R	E		S	L	I	D
P	E	R	T		N	A	M	E	S		C	I	N	E
T	A	D	A		S	P	E	L	L	C	H	E	C	K
S	T	U	R	G	E	O	N		S	E	G	U	E	
		W	E	A	N		T	O	P	L	E	S	S	
	C	H	A	R	M	S	C	H	O	O	L			
A	L	A	R	M		R	A	P	T		K	E	G	
D	O	G	S		P	A	I	N	S		H	A	V	E
O	D	S		P	A	C	E		E	E	R	I	E	
	W	A	R	T	S	A	N	D	A	L	L			
S	A	M	U	R	A	I		M	U	I	R			
A	C	E	R	S		B	I	R	T	H	D	A	Y	
C	U	R	S	E	W	O	R	D	S		E	I	R	E
C	R	I	T		O	B	E	S	E		A	K	I	N
O	A	T	S		K	E	A	T	S		R	E	D	S

75

M	A	R	T	I	N		A	W	L		P	A	R	S
A	P	I	E	C	E		L	I	E		U	T	A	H
P	R	O	T	E	S	T	A	N	T		G	A	T	E
L	I	T	E		T	A	M	E		P	E	R	S	E
E	L	S		R	E	F	O	R	M	A	T	I	O	N
		P	E	A	T		I	A	M	S				
H	I	J	A	B		A	E	R		O	A	T	S	
A	L	L	S	A	I	N	T	S	C	H	U	R	C	H
T	K	O	S		D	O	E		A	N	I	M	E	
		R	B	I	S		S	C	A	D				
I	N	D	U	L	G	E	N	C	E	S		F	A	R
B	O	O	S	T		D	O	O	R		O	L	G	A
S	I	G	H		W	I	T	T	E	N	B	E	R	G
E	S	M	E		A	V	E		A	H	I	S	E	E
N	E	A	R		Y	E	S		L	U	T	H	E	R